Dead for Nothing?

What the Cross Has Done for You

by
Phil Pringle

Harrison House
Tulsa, Oklahoma

Cover Design and Layout by Velvet Creative
www.velvet.com.au
Cover image "Cross" by Phil Pringle

10 09 08 07   10 9 8 7 6 5 4 3 2 1

Dead for Nothing?
What the Cross Has Done for You
ISBN 13: 978-1-57794-931-2
ISBN 10: 1-57794-931-5
Copyright 2003 by Pax Ministries Pty Ltd.
Locked Bag 8
Dee Why, NSW 2099
Australia
www.ccc.org.au

Published by Harrison House Publishers
P.O. Box 35035
Tulsa, Oklahoma 74153
www.harrisonhouse.com

Contents

Preface

"Back to the Cross!"

We've all heard a message or read an article along these lines at some time— and it's a good call. If we are distant from the Cross, then we need to make the journey back. The Cross is central to our Christianity. Yet I can't help thinking that the "Back to the Cross" message is too often presented as a morbid, solemn experience of deep reflection, remorse, and sorrow. Of course, this is important whenever we need to repent and get right with God. But repentance is a doorway. We don't live in a doorway; we live in a living room. And the living room is faith.

> To get back to the Cross is to get back to a life based on the death and resurrection of Jesus rather than one based on human effort.

There is much more to the work of the Cross than initially meets the eye. The Cross presents us with the singularly most powerful and enormous work of God in the earth. To get back to the Cross is to get back to a life—

an amazing life—based on the death and resurrection of Jesus rather than one based on human effort.

> We must take hold of truth and make our feelings embrace it. This is where the battle is.

We live in a day when unprecedented numbers of people around the world are asking Christ into their lives (various sources estimate about 120,000 daily). It is imperative that this great harvest of souls has its roots in the Word of God. In particular, they must discover and grasp the work Jesus has accomplished on the Cross.

It's amazing how many of us judge the effectiveness of the Cross by what our feelings tell us. If certain feelings fail to manifest in us, we conclude it can't be true, it doesn't work, or that God is not interested in us. This is wrong thinking. The truths of salvation are appropriated by a faith that acts.

Faith that acts was illustrated in the story of the Israelites possessing the Land of Canaan. The Promised Land has to be possessed—sometimes simply by walking into it, sometimes with a battle, but it must be appropriated. We appropriate truth by first gaining an understanding of what the

Word has promised and then aligning our emotions and thoughts with what God has stated.

We fail to appropriate and live in truth because we would rather have it all simply come to us without any effort. We want everything to feel good. However, if we wait for our feelings to tell us whether or not the Word is true we will be disappointed. Feelings, even positive ones, are not an accurate guide for living. Yet for many this is a normal way of life. For example, if we feel guilty rather than forgiven, we conclude that the truth must be that we are not forgiven. Why? Because we don't feel forgiven. We still feel guilty. But the Bible has declared us to be acquitted and justified!

> ...*being justified freely by His grace through the redemption that is in Christ Jesus....*
>
> ROMANS 3:24

We must take hold of truth and make our feelings embrace it. This is where the battle is. Our mind does not accept truth easily. It would rather take its information from the five senses than from the Word of God.

Paul says we are to pull down every high thought that exalts itself against the knowledge of God (2 Cor. 10:5). This means we (note that it's *we*, not God) pull down those thoughts that disagree with the Word. We make our mind conform to the Word of God (Rom. 12:2). We speak the Word into our thoughts.

Speaking the Word of God has enormous impact on our spiritual life. The Word is the sword of the Holy Spirit (Eph. 6:17). It is a double-edged sword (Heb. 4:12). It has a dual effect—it defeats the devil and builds our faith all in one action. We are told by the apostle to take up our spiritual armor (Eph. 6:13). Again, the onus is on us. The armor isn't placed on us; it is clothing that we take up and place on ourselves. The battle is won because we fight. And we fight with the sword of the Spirit, the Word of God.

What does it mean to appropriate truth? There's a lot of soap in the world, but there are still a lot of dirty people. Unless we use the soap it has no effect upon us. Truth is present. Learning to appropriate truth and live in it is the constant pursuit of the believer.

For YAH, the LORD, *is*
my strength and song;
He also has become
my salvation.

Isaiah 12:2

1

Salvation Through the Cross

*Behold, God **is** my salvation,*
I will trust and not be afraid;

*For Y*AH, *the L*ORD, **is** *my strength and song;*
He also has become my salvation.

Therefore with joy you will draw water
From the wells of salvation.

ISAIAH 12:2, 3

God has brought salvation to the earth through Jesus Christ, and this salvation came through the Cross. It is a complete salvation, a perfect salvation. Nothing can be added to it or taken from it (Heb. 7:27).

Many believers live in defeat because they haven't yet grasped the fullness of their salvation. We must realize that the work of the Cross has provided an absolutely complete salvation for the person who accepts Christ.

For some believers salvation relates only to being delivered from hell and gaining entrance to heaven. This is obviously a major part of the awesome work of the Cross, but it is not the only work. This "so great a salvation" (Heb. 2:3) encompasses deliverance from everything that destroys us and reveals how God loves us! He sent Jesus to save us from those things that threaten both our present wholeness and eternal well-being.

> This "so great a salvation" encompasses deliverance from everything that destroys us and reveals how God loves us!

Old Testament believers understood salvation in terms of deliverance from oppressive enemies, destructive circumstances, diseases, and disasters. Yahweh was their Savior who saved them from calamity. *The Holman Bible Dictionary* explains it like this.

"In the Old Testament, salvation primarily concerns God's saving acts within human history. The early prophets anticipated God's salvation to be realized in the earth's renewed fruitfulness and the rebuilding of the ruined cities of Israel. Salvation would extend to all nations who would stream to Zion for instruction in God's ways" (see Amos 9:13-15 and Isa. 2:2-4).

The Old Testament concept related more to the salvation of a community or a nation than to personal individual salvation.

This view of salvation has been expanded. New Testament salvation involves rescue from an eternal hell that awaits the wicked beyond this life. However, God's will for us in the "here and now" has not changed. He is still the deliverer. He is still the healer. He is still the provider of abundance. More specifically, He has provided these benefits through the work of Jesus on the Cross.

This is what we are exploring in this book—the seven great works of the Cross. Through the Cross we have been:

1. Set free from sin

2. Set free from sickness

3. Set free from the devil

4. Set free from poverty

5. Set free from the curse of the law

6. Set free from ourselves

7. Set free from the world

He breaks the power of cancelled sin.

—Charles Wesley

2

Sin No More

There is no other way to remove sin from the soul than through the blood of Jesus (1 Pet. 1:18-19). Sin separates people from God. The blood of Jesus reconciles us with God because sin is completely removed (Isa. 59:2). Through the work of the blood of Jesus our stained souls are washed whiter than snow (Col. 1:20).

Sin separates people from God.

We are completely set free from sin through Christ's death. God removes all sin, all iniquities, all trespasses, and all offenses. Everything keeping us from God has been removed by Jesus through His blood. The hymn writer Charles Wesley penned it brilliantly when he wrote, "He breaks the power of cancelled sin."

For sin shall not have dominion over you, for you are not under law but under grace.

ROMANS 6:14

> We think that if we can just be good enough, our sins will be atoned for, and we will be right with God.

The bowls on a bowling green all have a bias so that they veer to one side when bowled. This is like sin in us. We are born with a bias toward doing wrong and moving away from God. We don't have to teach children to do wrong, to lie, or to be mischievous. It comes naturally. This changes when we are born again. We receive a bias toward God. As we roll through life, we lean toward doing right, toward God.

Sin is the basis of all our problems. And yet, ignoring this fact, we seek solutions to our problems in a thousand other ways. If we fail to deal properly with sin, we will only continue struggling with unsolved problems. When we repent from sin and accept Christ, sin is erased from our soul, from our record before God, and from His memory. He declares,

> *"I, **even** I, **am** He who blots out your transgressions for My own sake; and I will not remember your sins."*

ISAIAH 43:25

It is a natural instinct for us to attempt to get right with God through our own effort. We think that if we can just be good enough, our sins will be atoned for (or at the very least overlooked), and we will be right with God. This kind of thinking might pacify our conscience, but our conscience is not God. Being right with God in heaven is an enormously different affair. Jesus died for us because our good works cannot save us or get us into right relationship with God.

The term "fallen from grace" is often applied when someone once considered a godly person has stumbled into an immoral lifestyle. But Scripture actually applies this term to those who have reverted to trying to gain salvation through their own effort, rather than relying on the work of Jesus to secure righteousness for them.

> *You have become estranged from Christ, you who attempt to be justified by law; you have fallen from grace.*
>
> GALATIANS 5:4

Today we are so unwilling to deal with our need to "face the music." We desperately seek to remove responsibility for our wrongdoing from ourselves. While we might stop short of using the "devil made me do it" excuse, we are effectively saying just that in a more sophisticated manner. "Dysfunctional behavior" is blamed on everything but ourselves.

"It's my genetic coding."

"It's the environment I was raised in."

"It's the way my grandmother treated my mother and my mother treated me."

"It's the tragedies I experienced as a child."

"It's the pressure of the situation I was in."

"I was so influenced by another person that I can't be held responsible for my actions."

Such arguments are all very convenient—until we ourselves become the mother or the father being blamed for the misdemeanors of our offspring!

> When we wrongly diagnose our problems, we prescribe the wrong answers.

In the Old Testament, if children committed serious crimes they could be stoned. Today, if children act up we stone the parents! And parents stone themselves believing that the behavior of their children is totally the result of how they have been raised. But every one of us is born with a propensity to sin. It's deep within our fallen nature to want to do wrong and to go ahead and do it. It takes a change of heart by the power of the Holy Spirit to make this different.

The only way to deal with sin is to repent from it and to be cleansed by the blood of Christ. But it is increasingly popular to think of wrongdoing as some kind of dysfunction or illness on the part of the person committing the wrongdoing. Criminals are often looked on with pity, even though they have committed terrible atrocities. You hear people say, "There's something faulty with the poor boy." As a result, their victims are shortchanged on compassion and feel justice has not been done.

Authorities speak of rehabilitation and healing and counseling. It is virtuous to extend pity and compassion, but this should not be done to the exclusion of justice. Some of the best rehabilitative processes involve making people face up to their crimes and accept the penalty due. If justice becomes "fallen," a deep cynicism about life develops in the community. When people feel that life is unfair, they develop deep frustrations. And the inevitable consequences of frustration are anger and violence.

When we wrongly diagnose our problems, we prescribe the wrong answers. Sin is not sickness. It cannot be healed. Many people are treated badly in their early developing

To repent is to accept responsibility for our actions.

years. Some are abused; others are ignored or abandoned; others are smothered by overprotective parents. All kinds of influences are at work in our lives. However, being able to explain why we behave badly doesn't excuse us—or heal us.

An explanation is neither an excuse nor a justification for evildoing. We still have the power of choice. We make decisions about how we respond to these events and circumstances in our lives. When we stand before the throne of God on Judgment Day, we will not be able to skirt neatly around the things we did by declaring, "It wasn't my fault! My genes made me do it."

Even if we have been somehow out of control at some stage and done things that were wrong, we still have to accept responsibility for the fact that it was we who did these things. This is the only way to rid ourselves of the impulse of sin within us. It is not a sickness; it is sin. Sin is a force we are born with. It drives us to do things that are wrong and offensive to God and people. The only way to deal with this force is through repentance and the blood of Jesus Christ.

Repentance begins by accepting responsibility for our actions then confessing our sin to the Father. If we don't accept responsibility for our actions, we will not be set free from the problem. It will recur. But once sin is dealt with, everything that gains a hold on our lives through sin becomes disabled. Sickness, demon possession, and curses are results of sin. When the foundation for their existence is gone, they can be dealt with properly.

> Repentance is taking sides with God against our carnal nature. When we can do this, we have found the key to freedom.

To repent is to accept responsibility for our actions. Our flesh does not want to do this. The devil diverts us. Well-meaning friends might try to relieve us from having to accept responsibility for our own behavior. But we must come into the light!

> *"For everyone practicing evil hates the light and does not come to the light, lest his deeds should be exposed. But he who does the truth comes to the light, that his deeds may be clearly seen, that they have been done in God."*
>
> JOHN 3:20-21

This is the first truth that is fundamental to the Christian life. If this does not happen when we are new believers, we will never find ourselves able to live a powerful Christian life. Life demands that we face uncomfortable situations. If we never gain the ability to come into the light—to be honest about ourselves and the situations that surround us—we will never build a great and successful life for God.

A basic premise for success in life is that we are able to face difficult circumstances—emotionally uncomfortable and conflicting encounters. Repentance is when we first learn to do this. It's uncomfortable to admit guilt and not to shift the blame, to accept full responsibility and shame. Repentance is taking sides with God against our carnal nature. When we can do this, we have found the key to freedom.

When we fail to accept responsibility for our actions, we inadvertently lose control of our lives. Although it is convenient to avoid an unpleasant emotional confrontation by claiming we were not really in control of our behavior, it is in so doing that we actually surrender control. If we take our hands off the wheel with regard to our past, then we have also taken our hands off the wheel for our present and future. It's the same wheel. Our past and our present powerfully influence our future.

Authority is inextricably entwined with responsibility. When we deny that we had any choice regarding our past actions, arguing that we had no control or no authority, we surrender the most priceless gift God has given us: the act of free will, the power of choice, and the authority to make decisions. The more we refuse to accept this, the more we reinforce our inability to take authority over our lives.

We must understand that God has already created an environment of forgiveness and mercy.

> *God was in Christ reconciling the world to Himself, not imputing their trespasses to them.*
>
> 2 CORINTHIANS 5:19

When Jesus was dying on the Cross, He was not condemning the world but bringing forgiveness and salvation to the world. He was not imputing our trespasses to us; He was reconciling us to God.

In Luke 15:20 we read that when the prodigal son returned home, his father was running to meet him. Taking into consideration that the father's reputation had been seriously maligned through his son's behavior, his father's action is even more striking. He had been left shorthanded on the farm. At least one third of his life's savings had been squandered by this renegade boy. His

> God has provided
> a safe environment
> of mercy—with
> forgiveness already
> given—for us
> to repent in.

feelings of disappointment over his son were high. His remorse over his own ability as a parent plagued him.

Given all this, it was perfectly reasonable for the prodigal to expect that the man running toward him would be anything but merciful. He was expecting his father to pull a gun out of his back pocket and begin firing. But the father kept running, and instead of producing some kind of weapon, he just held out his arms—to embrace him.

The father hugged and kissed the boy, and immediately the boy repented. He accepted full responsibility for his actions and begged to be received back into the family as a servant. The father promptly restored him to full sonship with all its privileges.

If the father had come with a gun, or even a pointing, accusing, shaking finger, the son would have offered a repentance that did not fully engage his heart. If we say we're sorry to someone who is already condemning us, and they carry on with their accusations even after we have confessed and offered our apologies, eventually we say something petulant like, "Well, I said I'm sorry. Take it or leave it!" This is not repentance. God has provided a safe environment of mercy—with forgiveness already given—for us to repent in.

Forgiveness is one of the greatest luxuries of life. To experience the Father's forgiveness and acceptance is enormous. The Greek word for forgiveness (*aphiemi*) means to loose, to set away, or to set free. Many of us fail to experience the forgiveness of God because we do not forgive ourselves.

God moves in our moving. Once we are aware of the will of God, we then need to implement it. We can give mental assent to a truth without letting it touch our lives at all. We must enact the Word of God. If we hear but fail to do, our "religion is in vain" (James 1:22).

When we stop roasting ourselves for past failures and forgive ourselves, we are enacting the Word of God. We then experience the forgiveness of God entering our lives. We also find it easier to forgive others once we have learned to forgive ourselves.

If God is prepared to forgive you, why can't you forgive yourself?

Forgiveness is the way of God. It accepts that we have done wrong, that we have violated a high moral expectation on ourselves, but also that there is mercy. Forgiveness doesn't justify or excuse a bad action; rather, when we seek forgiveness we find mercy.

We must have this merciful attitude in our own soul towards ourselves. Once the wall of self-judgment is broken, the bridge of self-forgiveness can be erected and God's forgiveness flows easily into our inner world so that we feel the forgiveness of God. This affects so many other areas.

If we live in self-loathing, we will be happy neither with ourselves nor with others. Although we might acknowledge the theory that God loves us, that's all it can be—a theory. We can't feel a thing! Once we forgive ourselves, however, we can move on to accepting ourselves and even liking or loving ourselves. Then we can feel a sense of worth. We can accept the worth God has placed on us.

A healthy self-image is a platform for God. He will speak words of comfort and encouragement to us constantly throughout our lives. But when we actually apply these things to ourselves, it releases the power of God to make His truths live in us. God never forces Himself on us. He moves through our moving. People need to be told not to be so hard on themselves.

If God is prepared to forgive you, why can't you forgive yourself?

Go ahead and tell yourself that you forgive yourself, just as God has forgiven you. Say it now. "I forgive myself. I will not hold my sins against myself any longer! Thank You, Lord, for helping me to forgive myself. Thank You for forgiving me. I accept it fully. Amen."

Guilt is one of the worst effects of sin. Our emotions are not built to carry guilt. Under the pressure of guilt we find ourselves doing things wrong and doing wrong things. When we feel uncomfortable because of guilt and are preoccupied with a sense of wrong, everybody and everything else become intrusions into our world. We react wrongly to people and events around us. Guilt dissolves as we accept forgiveness and cleansing from God.

The world attempts to remove guilt by legitimizing the wrong we did in the first place. It has long been a ploy of our fallen nature to escape repentance and the need to forsake doing wrong. Repentance involves not only accepting responsibility for our actions and confessing our sin to the Lord but also forsaking wrong.

> When we determine to turn from doing the wrong thing, God's power will accompany us in the effort.

*He who covers his sins will not prosper, but whoever
confesses and forsakes **them** will have mercy.*

PROVERBS 28:13

Besides telling us that we will never be successful if we
cover our sins, this scripture not only calls on us to confess
our sins but also to abandon them—to stop doing them.
When we determine to turn from doing the wrong thing,
God's power will accompany us in the effort.

Part of the process of making the decision to no longer
continue in sin is actually to correct our past. Repentance
involves making right that which is wrong. This is founda-
tional to building strength of character. It is the basis of
integrity. No one will live a perfect life. When we do fall, we
must be prepared to face the music and put things right.
This is challenging, difficult, and uncomfortable, but if we
are to walk in the light we must be committed to this.

Restitution should also take place within the circle of
offense. If I have offended a particular person, then I need
to make it right with that person. It is not necessary for
me to confess my failure to anyone else. If I have had critical thoughts or bad attitudes toward others, then I need to
confess that only to God. If the people concerned are
unaware of my difficulties, it is only an added burden to
their life if I load them up with my problems.

Stolen goods should be returned as well. Zacchaeus returned four times more than he had wrongly taken from his own people (Luke 19:8). His sense of making right his wrongs was strong and he was determined to please God.

Whatever it means to put things right, we should do it. It may mean writing a letter of apology, straightening crooked business practices, or admitting to lies or cheating. All these things lay a foundation for a powerful, immovable life. This is a very difficult truth for some, but without it we build a house that will fall when the storms come. A clear conscience is the secret to a bold life. When there are no skeletons in the closet we won't be checking over our shoulder for the rest of our days.

God moves in our moving. Once our will is set in motion, we can expect the power of God to assist us. Even though at times we may slip and fall in our pursuit of forsaking sin, the blood of Christ is still effective to cleanse us.

> *Though he fall, he shall not be utterly cast down;*
> *For the LORD upholds **him with** His hand.*
>
> PSALM 37:24

Even though we may sometimes feel disappointed with ourselves, we are not to run from God when we fall, but rather we are to run to Him.

God fully understands our flesh and our propensity towards sin, so He has made provision for this in the New Covenant.

*If we confess our sins, He is faithful and just to forgive **us** **our** sins and to cleanse us from all unrighteousness.*

1 JOHN 1:9

The blood of Christ is not just effective when we first come to Christ and receive salvation. We will need it many times throughout our Christian life. Even though we may sometimes feel disappointed with ourselves, we are not to run *from* God when we fall, but rather we are to run *to* Him.

The impulse to sin, the motivation towards evil, has been destroyed through the Cross.

When Jesus attempted to wash Peter's feet (John 13:10), He told Peter that even though he was completely washed, he still needed to have his feet washed. The picture Jesus was creating for the disciples here alludes to Roman public baths. People would wash in the public baths and then return home. On the way home, however, their feet would become dirty again. So arriving home they would wash their feet.

This is like the Christian walk. When we first meet Christ, He washes us completely clean. We receive salvation and acceptance into the family of God. As we travel through life, however, there are times when we offend God (1 John 1:8). At these points we must repent, confess, and turn from our offenses again. We are promised that the blood of Jesus will cleanse us again so that sin and all the curses that come with it will not stick to our lives (1 John 1:9).

This is the great work of the Cross. God, through grace, has provided a means for regular cleansing and renewing of our relationship with Him. Thus is the manifested power of the Cross in our lives. Repentance is how we apply the blood of Christ to our souls and find the power of cleansing and forgiveness through the blood of the Lamb.

In Romans 6:14 Paul tells us that sin no longer has dominion over us. That's because the force of sin has been destroyed in Christ. The impulse to sin, the motivation toward evil, has been destroyed through the Cross. Jesus has not only forgiven us for the sins we have committed, but also He has brought death to sin itself. He actually became sin for us (2 Cor. 5:21) and in dying put sin itself to death. Therefore, whoever receives Him receives the death of sin and the power of righteousness into their lives.

If Jesus has borne our sicknesses,
then we no longer need to bear them.

3

The End of Sickness

...*who Himself bore our sins in His own body on the tree, that we, having died to sins, might live for righteousness; by whose stripes you were healed.*

1 PETER 2:24

The Living Bible says, "For his wounds have healed ours!" Jesus has taken our sicknesses upon Himself so that we do not have to bear them ourselves.

...*that it might be fulfilled which was spoken by Isaiah the prophet, saying:*

"He Himself took our infirmities and bore our sicknesses."

MATTHEW 8:17

> The Cross is the basis for wholeness. When Jesus took our sins away, He also took our diseases away.

If Jesus has borne our sicknesses, then we no longer need to bear them. Healing is ours through the work of the Cross. The Cross is the basis for wholeness. When Jesus took our sins away, He also took our diseases away.

Since the book of Genesis, God has revealed Himself as the ultimate healer. When He manifested in the flesh as Jesus, it was completely in keeping with His divine nature to heal sickness. It has always been the will of God to heal sickness. Whenever He sees sickness, it's His nature to heal it.

He revealed Himself as the healer of Israel through His name Jehovah Rapha—"The Lord who heals you" (Ex. 15:26). The Lord established the fact that if the Israelites would destroy the false gods of the surrounding nations and serve Him exclusively, then He would ensure that sickness was removed from their lives.

"I will take sickness away from the midst of you."

EXODUS 23:25

Healing comes time and time again throughout the Old Testament with the Atonement, intercession, and the Passover sacrifices. In Genesis 20:17, Abraham intercedes for the house of Abimilech, and all the women are healed of barrenness.

When the Israelites left Egypt, each household sacrificed a lamb. After this there was not a sick one among them as they marched out of bondage (Ps. 105:37).

When the Israelites were bitten by a plague of snakes in the desert, Moses lifted up a brass likeness of a snake on a pole, and anyone who looked at it was healed (Num. 21:8-9). Jesus later referred to this as being exactly what was to happen to Him—that He too would be lifted up. It follows that whomever looks to the Cross will discover healing (John 3:14).

Through the fall we lost everything. Through the Cross Jesus recovered everything.

In Leviticus 14 we read of the priests placing the blood of a sacrifice on a leper. Once the ceremony was complete the leper was cleansed. Healing took place as the person received the blood of the sacrifice. Since leprosy has always been a symbol of sin, besides demonstrating the actual healing of the disease, the cleansing of the leprosy is a symbol of the cleansing of sin.

When Hezekiah kept the Passover in 2 Chronicles 30:20, "The Lord listened to Hezekiah and healed the people." In 1 Corinthians 11:30 Paul tells the believers they are weak and sickly because they have failed to esteem correctly the Lord's Supper. Some were partaking of it unworthily because of attitudes and lifestyles that were unacceptable to the Lord. Others who were sick were failing to appropriate the work of the Cross into their lives.

All of these examples show us that healing and the Atonement are connected.

Through the fall we lost everything. Through the Cross Jesus recovered everything. Salvation of any aspect of humanity without sacrifice, without the shedding of blood, is unknown in Scripture.

Dr. Young, author of *Young's Analytical Concordance,* translates Isaiah 53:4-5 as follows: "Surely our sickness (Hebrew—*choli*) He has borne, and our pains He has carried them...and by His bruise there is healing for us."

Dr. Isaac Leeser, translator of the *Hebrew English Bible,* renders these verses as, "He was despised and shunned by men; A man of pains and acquainted with disease. But only our diseases did He bear Himself, and our pains He carried."

Faith makes real the promises of God.

When Jesus was crucified, He was dealing with more than just sin. He was also providing the basis for healing and delivering people from sickness. Many times freedom from sin and healing from sickness are placed side by side. For example, the psalmist declares,

> *Who* [the Lord] *forgives all your iniquities,*
> *Who heals all your diseases.*
>
> PSALM 103:3 [brackets mine]

In the forgiveness of sin there is also the healing of diseases. God is not limited to forgiving only a few select sins. He forgives ALL sins. The same applies to disease—He heals ALL diseases. There is no disease that God is incapable of healing. Jesus saw little difference between setting a person free from their sin and setting them free from their sickness.

> *"For which is easier, to say, '****Your**** sins are forgiven you,' or to say, 'Arise and walk'? But that you may know that the Son of Man has power on earth to forgive sins"—then He said to the paralytic, "Arise, take up your bed, and go to your house."*
>
> MATTHEW 9:5-6

The man was immediately healed. Jesus demonstrated that healing and forgiveness of sin work together.

To discover the power of the Cross for healing, we must understand how to appropriate truth. If it were a meal on a plate we could eat it. If it were an item in a store we could purchase it. If it were fruit on a tree we could pluck it. Even though these may serve well as spiritual metaphors, we are always in need of knowing how to make spiritual truths physical realities in our world. The bridge between the two is always faith. Faith makes real the promises of God.

Faith is released when there is total confidence that something is in the will of God. Healing is, always has been, and always will be the will of God. He never changes. He's the same yesterday, today, and forever (Heb. 13:8). Jesus demonstrated this. He is the express image of God in the earth (Heb. 1:3). He is the perfect revelation of the will of God. He is the character of God manifested to us.

Not once do we find Jesus laying His hands on anyone to make them sick. The very suggestion verges on blasphemy. He healed only the sick. Acts 10:38 tells us that it is the devil who damages people and Jesus who makes them whole. When Jesus was asked if He would heal sick people, His answer was, "Yes!" (Matt. 8:2-3).

Jesus is no respecter of persons (Acts 10:34). What He has done for others, He will do for you and me. He healed all who went to Him (Matt. 8:16). Few doubt His ability to heal. But many are uncertain of His willingness to heal them. If He has healed others, why would He not heal you or me? We are neither better nor worse than those God has touched in other times.

Faith always starts with desire. We want something to happen. Faith always wants a thing enough to do whatever it takes. Faith begins with a desire strong enough to make you determined to make it happen. There is more.

Faith decides it will get it. Faith is determined. It makes its mind up. It is not double-minded. The decision is made—I'm going to get healed. I don't entertain, "But what if?" The decision is made—I'm committed.

Faith asks God to make it happen. Faith cries out to God no matter what pressures there are to block us. Faith persists. It doesn't give up because of a few disappointments. It keeps on asking. It does not allow its heart to be discouraged. Discouragement is one of the worst enemies of faith. It is imperative to rise above every rejection and to persevere until the answer is there.

Faith is certain of a miracle. It knows God is involved. It doesn't pretend. Faith is an inner, clear knowledge and revelation of realities that are not evident to the natural senses. Faith is so certain of those realities that it acts as though they are true—simply because they are. It makes decisions based on those certainties. It plans according to what it knows.

> Faith acts.
> Without action
> faith is dead.
> Real faith
> always acts.

Faith speaks of those realities as finished acts. It says, "Thank You, Lord. It's already done," "It has already happened," "I've got it right now," "God has done it." Faith always speaks. It's faith's first reaction. If we believe a thing, we speak it. It's not necessarily loud; it doesn't rely on volume or excitement, but rather on the power of God's Word.

Faith knows God as faithful.

Faith speaks the promises of God and refuses to speak things that oppose the promises.

Faith acknowledges truth rather than facts.

Faith connects the promises of God with the desires of the heart.

Faith gives glory to God for things not yet manifest.

Faith knows that things are built in the spirit first and then fall into the natural.

Faith is a creative force; that's why it speaks just as God does when He creates.

The Word of the Lord and healing go together. He created the world through His Word.

Speak the Word

Faith sees realities not seen by natural eyes. It can see healing as having already happened. It can feel the emotions of the experience because it's there in the future, in full view of the realities of the answer. Faith spends time meditating on that vision. It doesn't imagine disaster; it sees the answer.

Faith acts. Without action faith is dead. Real faith always acts. Faith does not care what obstacles there are. It surmounts them to receive the answer. Four men lift off a roof to lower their friend into the presence of Jesus, and the paralyzed man is healed. Bartimaeus ignores the crowd trying to silence his cry for help, and Jesus hears him, calls him, and heals him.

The Canaanite woman presses through the apparent reluctance of Jesus to heal her daughter. The disciples have pushed her back. Jesus has first ignored her and then told her that she doesn't qualify for a miracle because she is a foreigner. But she keeps coming in spite of all this and she gets her miracle.

In just the same way as the Father has provided forgiveness for His children, He has also provided healing for all. God has arranged for this healing to travel into our lives by several different means. But even though He employs a variety of ways to impart healing, it is always based on two things: First, healing has been secured for us through the death of Christ on the Cross; second, faith is always essential to the equation. Faith is the currency of heaven. Faith on the part of the person praying, faith of the sufferer, or faith expressed by others releases the power of God bringing healing.

Laying on of Hands

Healing is imparted through the laying on of hands.

"They will lay hands on the sick, and they will recover."

MARK 16:18

Through the laying on of hands God is imparted to people. Healing from God is a supernatural flow of the life of God. Healing is spiritual life. This "life" is not nothing. We must understand that God is not nothing—God is something. God is spirit, and spirit is something.

*God **is** Spirit.*

JOHN 4:24

For want of a better term, God is "stuff." Spirit is not nothing. Spirit is a substance, albeit a spiritual one. Spirit substance cannot be seen with physical eyes, felt with our physical body, heard with physical ears, or smelled or tasted with our nose or mouth. Our physical bodies are not equipped to perceive the spirit realm. Spirit relates to spirit. Flesh relates to flesh.

That which is born of the flesh is flesh, and that which is born of the Spirit is spirit.

JOHN 3:6

*For those who live according to the flesh set their minds on the things of the flesh, but those **who live** according to the Spirit, the things of the Spirit.*

ROMANS 8:5

We, however, are spiritual beings. Our spiritual nature finds expression through our physical bodies. We are "temples" of the Holy Spirit (1 Cor. 3:16). Our own spirits live within us (Dan. 7:15). The Father and Jesus dwell within us (John 14:23). These are all spiritual entities.

> The "stuff" of God gets into things and works miracles. It changes lives, heals sicknesses, and causes evil spirits to leave. It is the Spirit of God.

Spiritual life can be imparted from one person to another, from one thing to another. This happens through the laying on of hands. While this applies to many areas other than just healing, healing is a primary application of the laying on of hands. The "stuff" of God travels from one person to another through the laying on of hands.

This "stuff" can actually permeate physical things. Spiritual life can get inside physical things. Paul laid his hands on cloth, and when it was laid on sick people, whatever had gotten into the cloth was released into the sufferers' bodies and they were healed.

> ...so that even handkerchiefs or aprons were brought from his body to the sick, and the diseases left them and the evil spirits went out of them.
>
> ACTS 19:12

This miraculous power resides inside the physical body. We tend to imagine that because spirit is nonphysical it is somehow separate from our body. We imagine that we are like a hollow case and that our spirit dwells in the hollow.

This is not at all the case. The spiritual life of God actually infuses our physical bodies. This life of God gets inside our flesh and our bones. This is where the healing life of God—the "stuff" of God himself—lives.

Some time after the miracle-working prophet Elisha was dead and buried, bands of Moab raiders invaded Israel. During one of the battles, the soldiers were attempting to bury one of their fellows but the raiders attacked them. In their haste the soldiers threw the dead man into the tomb of Elisha. The bones of the prophet had become exposed. As soon as the dead man landed on the bones of Elisha he revived. He was resurrected by the power of God that was still resident in the bones of a dead man who had once worked miracles through the power of God.

> So it was, as they were burying a man, that suddenly they spied a band **of raiders;** and they put the man in the tomb of Elisha; and when the man was let down and touched the bones of Elisha, he revived and stood on his feet.
>
> 2 KINGS 13:21

The power of God lives in our flesh and bones. It lives in physical things. The presence of God permeates buildings and atmospheres. It infuses our bodies and our workplaces. The "stuff" of God gets into things and works miracles. It changes lives, heals sicknesses, and causes evil spirits to leave. It is the Spirit of God. No evil spirit can remain wherever the power of God and the Holy Spirit take up residence. When light comes, darkness goes.

This "stuff" is imparted through the laying on of hands. It travels from one person to another as we lay on hands with that purpose in mind. It flows through the spiritual atmosphere of faith and it seems to matter little who it is that actually expresses that faith.

It can be the friends or relatives of a sufferer.

> *Then behold, they brought to Him a paralytic lying on a bed. When Jesus saw their faith, He said to the paralytic, "Son, be of good cheer; your sins are forgiven you."*
>
> MATTHEW 9:2

> *While He spoke these things to them, behold, a ruler came and worshiped Him, saying, "My daughter has just died, but come and lay Your hand on her and she will live."*
>
> MATTHEW 9:18

It can be the faith of the sufferers themselves.

> *Then He touched their eyes, saying, "According to your faith let it be to you."*
>
> MATTHEW 9:29

It can be the faith of the one ministering the healing.

Then Jesus answered and said, "O faithless and perverse generation, how long shall I be with you? How long shall I bear with you? Bring him here to Me."

MATTHEW 17:17

If faith is absent and there is an active atmosphere of unbelief, the release and flow of this life of God is severely restricted. Even Jesus himself found the release of power was restricted when unbelief prevailed.

As we pray fervently and effectively for one another, we bring healing to the church.

Now He could do no mighty work there, except that He laid His hands on a few sick people and healed **them.** *And He marveled because of their unbelief.*

MARK 6:5-6

The Gift of Healing

...to another [is given] *gifts of healings by the same Spirit....*

1 CORINTHIANS 12:9 [brackets mine]

Some people in the church are especially gifted by the Holy Spirit to impart healing. They have a gift to heal sick people. All Christians can pray with an expectation for people to be healed (James 5:16), but there are definitely certain people who are particularly gifted by God to minister healing to the sick.

This gift is also their calling and motivation. They approach the entire gospel from the perspective of healing. The revelation and insight of these people naturally travels down the line of healing sicknesses. Again, this gift is generally imparted through the laying on of hands.

Note that 1 Corinthians 12:8 speaks of healing gifts in plural terms. Because there are so many kinds of sicknesses, it seems that God gives people giftings to heal particular diseases. This arouses higher levels of faith for people with those particular sicknesses.

People Are Healed As Others Join Together and Pray for Them

Confess your trespasses to one another, and pray for one another, that you may be healed. The effective, fervent prayer of a righteous man avails much.

JAMES 5:16

When we pray for others we are interceding. We are standing in the gap. We are taking on their problem as though it were ours. We are standing before God on their behalf. Intercession gets results. As we pray fervently and effectively for one another, we bring healing to the church.

When I was a young assistant minister, a young boy who was suffering around twenty-four epileptic seizures every day was brought to me. His parents expected healing. He was becoming cut, bruised, and badly damaged. I felt so sorry for this young kid and for his parents, who were great people. The pressure on them was becoming unbearable.

I took the matter to our midweek church meeting. We joined hands around the auditorium and began praying. A great spirit of prayer came upon us, and we rose into a realm of prayer and intercession I had never experienced before.

After a little while it seemed we had prayed for long enough. A general feeling of rest from crying out to God had come into the room. However, the Lord said to me, "Rise again. You're not through yet." So I told the people to rest for a few moments, and then we rose again in prayer.

> As people believe the Word, healing enters their lives or the life of the one they are bringing to the Lord.

After only about ten minutes, the stamina of the people began to flag again. This kind of intercessory prayer is very exacting. The spiritual stamina of most people in prayer is not great. Even in worship, most people can hold their position for only about five minutes before their spirit tires and they lose emotional and mental focus.

I felt we had still not yet broken through. We sang a quiet song in worship to strengthen our spirits, and then we prayed a third time. This time as we reached a crescendo, there was a definite "crack" in the spirit. We had broken through. People were clapping, shouting, and jumping up and down. We had a deep witness that something powerful had happened.

I rang the parents of the young boy the next day. They told me he had had only four seizures that day. The following day he had none at all.

Healing travels through prayer.

The Word of God Heals People

The Word of God is a miracle-working healing force in the earth.

He sent His word and healed them.

PSALM 107:20

In the Gospels, Jesus often does not go to the sufferer but rather simply speaks the Word and the miracle happens (Matt. 8:4). As people believe the Word, healing enters their lives or the life of the one they are bringing to the Lord.

A friend of mine was diagnosed with cancer. The tumor was about the size of an orange under his ribs and arm. His wife wouldn't allow anyone to speak anything negative anywhere in his room. She wouldn't allow anyone she thought might speak negative things to visit him. They plastered the walls of his hospital room with scriptures and began speaking the Word of God day and night. When he was finally operated on, they found the cancer was completely dead. Instead of him who was dying, the cancer had died!

Jesus lives and so do those who believe Him.

Jesus heals. He works miracles. And so do those who believe Him.

I have a list of scriptures I often give people and it's called "prescription promises." The power of the Word of God is severely underestimated. The prophets Elijah and Elisha simply spoke the Word of God and, one after another, awesome miracles took place. Jesus spoke the Word to impossible situations time and again, and the Word they all spoke carried healing and miracles into people's lives.

The Word of God is a miracle-working healing force in the earth.

> For [my words] **are** life to those who find them,
> And health to all their flesh.
>
> PROVERBS 4:22 [brackets mine]

Paul tells us we've been set free from the devil through the work of the Cross.

Revelation of the Word of God is the Word being unpacked into our spirits. Revelation is light. It is truth entering our inner being. Revelation is the food of the spirit. Revelation of the Word of God is an actual life force that travels into our spirits. It is imparted when we speak it.

The Word of God is a creative force. God created all that is with His Word. The power of His Word has not been diminished one iota. The same power is active in His Word now as was in His Word at the creation of the earth and the entire universe.

When the Word enters our spirit it comes as light. It is power that can be imparted. It is "stuff" that can be sent into people's bodies and into situations to bring miracles and solutions. It is the life of God.

...that at the name of Jesus
every knee should bow,
of those in heaven,
and of those on earth,
and of those under the earth....

Philippians 2:10

4

A Defeated Foe

How many Christians constantly complain about the devil doing things in their lives? They seem to be completely overrun by devils attacking them all the time. This is not the position of a New Testament believer. Paul tells us we've been set free from the devil through the work of the Cross.

Having disarmed principalities and powers, He made a public spectacle of them, triumphing over them in it.

COLOSSIANS 2:15

This refers to the fact that Jesus has defeated the devil in hell and publicly displayed this to every demon in the realms of darkness.

The conflict Jesus had with the devil was predicted right from the start in the Garden of Eden.

"I will put enmity
Between you and the woman,
And between your seed and her Seed;
He shall bruise your head,
And you shall bruise His heel."

GENESIS 3:15

Jesus himself revealed the principle by which He releases people from the grip of Satan—first He binds the devil, then He takes those who have been held captive.

This prophecy declared that there was to be a battle where the devil would bruise the heel of Jesus, but Jesus would bruise the head of Satan. In other words Jesus would bring His heel down heavily on the head of the devil. For that to happen, the devil would have to be on the ground, defeated in a battle.

David also prophesied that Jesus would take captives in His ascension from the grave.

When you ascended on high,
you led captives in your train.

PSALM 68:18 NIV

Isaiah also predicted the battle Jesus had to have, and the spoils of His victory would be shared.

Therefore I will give him a portion among the great,
and he will divide the spoils with the strong,
because he poured out his life unto death,
and was numbered with the transgressors.
For he bore the sin of many,
and made intercession for the transgressors.

ISAIAH 53:12 NIV

Jesus himself revealed the principle by which He releases people from the grip of Satan—first He binds the devil, then He takes those who have been held captive.

"Or again, how can anyone enter a strong man's house and carry off his possessions unless he first ties up the strong man? Then he can rob his house."

MATTHEW 12:29 NIV

But when someone stronger attacks and overpowers him, he takes away the armor in which the man trusted and divides up the spoils.

LUKE 11:22 NIV

Jesus realized He had both to bind the strong man and to remove his entire armor before He could take his possessions. When He died He went first to the presence of God and then into the

He paraded the devil defeated, bound, hobbled, and stripped of authority.

regions of hell where He entered into a conflict with the devil (Luke 23:46; Ecc. 12:7; 1 Pet. 3:19; Rev. 1:18).

When Peter says that Jesus preached to the spirits, the word he uses (*kerusso*) means "to herald as a public crier." The public crier was the person who announced news that affected everyone in a town. A trumpet would sound to gain the people's attention, then a royal proclamation or some other message would be shouted out by the town crier. In the absence of radio, television, fax, telephone, or computers, this was the only method of communicating to a large number of people at any given time.

After Jesus defeated Satan in an enormous battle in hell, He made a spectacle of the devil to all the demons and angels. He paraded the devil defeated, bound, hobbled, and stripped of authority. He led the devil past all the cohorts of the evil one in the corridors of Hades. Jesus then announced to all the devils in hell that He now held the keys to hell and death, and whenever any demon heard His name spoken by a believer, they must bow and obey.

At the name of Jesus every knee should bow, of those in heaven, and of those on earth, and of those under the earth.

PHILIPPIANS 2:10

Jesus' preaching was the announcement of His victory. After three days He was victorious, having completely disarmed the devil (Col. 2:15). All the weapons and armor in which the devil trusted were stripped from him.

The *Believers Study Bible* says of Colossians 2:15 that the "public display" Jesus made of the devil was a picture drawn from the triumphant Roman general who would strip his foes and lead them as captives behind his chariot in a victory procession through the streets of Rome before Caesar. The captured foes and all their nobles were often stripped naked and hobbled, shuffling along behind the chariot of the victorious general so that their humiliation was complete.

> The only legal foothold the devil has for access to and control over humans is sin.

The power of sin was completely annihilated through the blood of Christ. Because Jesus fulfilled and superseded the law, the devil could no longer accuse people by means of the law. Christ took away all grounds for any accusation against a person by bringing forgiveness, acceptance, and justification through the work of the Cross. The power of death, sickness, and sin was removed from the devil

He would take poverty to the Cross and secure its defeat for those who would embrace Him as Savior.

because the pure Christ of heaven could not be contained in hell (Acts 2:24).

The only legal foothold the devil has for access to and control over humans is sin. Sin is his doorway into the human soul. But Jesus slammed the door shut in the devil's face when He removed sin through the Cross. Satan no longer has any way of gaining access into a person's life if they are in Christ. Obviously, the benefits of the Cross apply only if we have accepted Christ and believed the gospel.

For you know the grace of our
Lord Jesus Christ,
that though He was rich,
yet for your sakes He became poor,
that you through His poverty
might become rich.

2 Corinthians 8:9

5

Poverty Abolished

In 2 Corinthians 8:9, Paul refers to the fact that Jesus Christ died without a single possession to His name, without a stitch of clothing on His body, and without any money at all. In this way He would take poverty to the Cross and secure its defeat for those who would embrace Him as Savior.

> *For you know the grace of our Lord Jesus Christ, that though He was rich, yet for your sakes He became poor, that you through His poverty might become rich.*
>
> 2 CORINTHIANS 8:9

This scripture is found right in the middle of two chapters written to the Corinthians that deal almost exclusively with the subject of money. Many commentators have great difficulty admitting that this passage is actually about money. In fact, I don't think I've found one yet who agrees that Paul is speaking specifically about finances here. The most common comment is that Paul is referring to spiritual riches.

The *Thompson Chain Reference Bible* is a wonderful resource and study Bible, but even it identifies what Paul is referring to as "spiritual riches." *Jamieson, Fausset and Brown* come closest in their commentary when they talk about "the heavenly glory which constitutes His riches, and all other things, so far as are really good for us."

Matthew Henry interprets "rich" as meaning "rich in the love of God, rich in the blessings of the New Covenant, rich in the hopes of eternal life." The *Word Biblical Commentary*, claiming the authorship of a team of respected international scholars and described as "a showcase of the best in evangelical critical scholarship for a new generation," states the following regarding this verse:

> Here, surely wealth and poverty are ciphers, not for material prosperity and penury but for spiritual exchange as the Incarnate Christ became what we are, so we could become what He is.

But for that to be consistent, the verse would have to read, "Christ...became spiritually poor that you might become spiritually rich." This becomes an absurd, almost blasphemous, proposition. To suggest or even intimate that Jesus Christ was a spiritually poor person is ludicrous. Here is a person who raised the dead, healed the sick, displayed complete prowess over demons and the devil, and revealed profound truths regarding God, humanity, and the entire purpose of God—truths that have withstood every kind of test and scrutiny.

The devil's scheme has been to deceive the church into believing that it is far more pious to be poor than it is to be rich.

Jesus was no spiritually poor person. Rather, it was by virtue of His spiritual wealth that He was able to go to the Cross and bear away the curses that afflict humankind. Even if we were to limit His poverty to the time He was on the Cross, claiming it was our poverty that He took on, are we to conclude that the "hope" He entered into (Acts 2:26) was a spiritually poor position? To have been able to maintain any kind of hope and faith throughout His ordeal demonstrates an extraordinary spiritual richness on the part of Jesus.

By trying to read more into Paul's statement than is actually there, we make fools of ourselves and prevent God from fulfilling His great promises in our lives. Jesus became poor

The kind of thinking that argues that high spirituality comes only at the expense of physical blessing defrauds the believer of their inheritance.

on the Cross with respect to the wealth of this world that those who receive Him may become rich with the wealth of this world.

Many people (mostly Christians) have a terrible amount of trouble accepting this fact. The devil's scheme has been to deceive the church into believing that it is far more pious to be poor than it is to be rich. Suspicion is cast upon those who have accumulated wealth. God is seen as one who would rather His people be poor than enjoy abundance in their world. But abundance has always been the will of God for His people.

Getting over a poverty mindset, however, is a lot more difficult than most people realize. A spirit of religiosity is at the root of this consciousness. As early as the first century, Paul encountered it when dealing with the errors of the Colossian church.

*Let no one cheat you of your reward, taking delight in **false** humility and worship of angels, intruding into those things which he has not seen, vainly puffed up by his fleshly mind.*

COLOSSIANS 2:18

The religious spirit enjoys being ascetic because it draws pride from the effort. This kind of spiritual indulgence actually only severs a person from Christ. Just as Esau was cheated out of his inheritance, so believers can be cheated out of theirs. Asceticism (self-inflicted austerity and poverty), posing as spirituality, cheats believers out of all the blessings Christ won for them through the work of the Cross.

> God wants us to think bigger than we have ever thought before.

The kind of thinking that argues that high spirituality comes only at the expense of physical blessing defrauds the believer of their inheritance. The Word of God, on the other hand, causes us to gain it (Acts 20:32). Paul describes a spirituality that poses as Christianity as involving false humility. The word "humility" here is translated from Greek words that mean "depressed, that is figuratively speaking, humiliated in circumstances or disposition, not joyful but base, cast down, humble, of low degree and estate."

We are called to humility, but not to a servility that embraces poverty and depression as though it were a piety that pleases the Father.

The other word for this "humility" (*tapeinophrosune*) is taken from the root *phren* meaning "to reign in the midriff"; that is, figuratively speaking, reigning in the feelings and heart and by extension the mind and understanding (cognitive abilities) as well. This, then, is saying that the religious spirit promotes smallness (the reigning in) of feelings and mind as if this pleases God. But in actual fact, it only cheats us out of our inheritance in Christ.

The church has been notorious for small, poor, and backward thinking, and justifying it because it is "for the Lord." This is to say that we should do things in a small and second-rate way because we are doing it for the Lord. This is ridiculous. God wants us to think bigger than we have ever thought before. We are not to limit God with our thinking; rather, we need to release Him with ever-increasing largeness of thinking and by dreaming of doing great exploits for Him.

> God believed that Job would remain true to Him, no matter what happened to him, whether he had everything or nothing.

Right from the start those who have pleased God have enjoyed abundance in their lives. Abraham became exceedingly prosperous as he obeyed God.

*Abram **was** very rich in livestock, in silver, and in gold.*

GENESIS 13:2

His son Isaac also prospered as the blessing of abundance promised to Abraham also came upon his descendants.

Then Isaac sowed in that land, and reaped in the same year a hundredfold; and the LORD blessed him. The man began to prosper, and continued prospering until he became very prosperous; for he had possessions of flocks and possessions of herds and a great number of servants. So the Philistines envied him.

GENESIS 26:12-14

These people recognized the blessing of God was on their lives because God had blessed them. The sons of Isaac were also blessed. As Jacob honored God in tithing as his grandfather Abraham had, he received a great abundance from the Lord.

"Jacob...has acquired all this wealth."

GENESIS 31:1

Even Job, who lived around the time of Abraham, was very wealthy. In fact, he was considered to be the wealthiest man in the East.

> The life we have in Christ is meant to be an abundant one at every level.

Also, his possessions were seven thousand sheep, three thousand camels, five hundred yoke of oxen, five hundred female donkeys, and a very large household, so that this man was the greatest of all the people of the East.

JOB 1:3

This is the man God was willing to challenge the devil over. God believed that Job would remain true to Him, no matter what happened to him, whether he had everything or nothing. The devil was granted permission to afflict Job with some of the worst sufferings we could imagine, yet Job did remain true to the Lord. His wealth had not corrupted his soul but rather had increased his sensitivity to the needs of those around him.

Moses and Aaron received the tithes of all the priests who had received the tithes of all the people (Num. 18:28). There were 600,000 men in Israel at that time. If we were to give two-thirds of them employment at $250 a week, that amounts to a $25 tithe multiplied by 400,000, which equals $10 million a week. The tithe of this is $1 million. That's what Moses and his brother would have received (Num. 18:26)—about $52 million a year! This goes to show just how small our current-day thinking is in this area. We would have to agree that the figures in these equations are conservative in today's world.

Some might say, "But that was while they were wandering in the wilderness and had nothing much anyway." But that is ridiculous thinking. They had literally plundered Egypt on the way out, and the laws Moses was instituting were intended for when they entered Canaan. They were meant to enter Canaan shortly after they had departed from Egypt, but the Israelites were waylaid by their own unbelief at the sight of giants in the land.

God had the largest people on earth build the mightiest cities and plant the greatest farmlands in some of the best climate on the planet—all for His people, Israel. All they had to do was go in and take it. The only difficulty they would face was the need to oust the giants. But God would be with them and the whole exercise was to be reasonably easy. However, they stumbled in their faith, and as a result, they wandered in the wilderness for forty years, not experiencing the abundance the Father had already prepared for them.

This is much like the church in many areas today. We have seen "giants" in the land and have been scared off from going in and taking what God has prepared for us. The life we have in Christ is meant to be an abundant one at every level. We are not saved to become paupers in the earth. Jesus died to set us free from poverty.

King David was also extraordinarily wealthy, so much so that he was able to give over $2.8 billion in gold, over and above his regular offerings, for the building of the temple (1 Chron. 29:3-4). Twenty-two times David refers to the offerings he brought into the house of God, his tithing, and the fulfillment of the pledges he had made to God. All this is part of the process by which the Lord brings blessing upon our lives.

King Solomon, the son of King David, invited the Queen of Sheba to his palace. She herself was extremely wealthy, but her breath was taken away when she saw the expanse of the wealth of Solomon (1 Kings 10).

Even the prophets were not considered poor. Isaiah is considered to have come from a wealthy background, Jonah had enough money to purchase a ticket on a boat to a distant country, and Jeremiah was readily able to go out and buy an acreage for 17 shekels (about $9,000—one shekel being the equivalent of four-days' wages) when the Lord told him to (Jer. 32:9).

Jesus himself received gold, frankincense, and myrrh at his birth. From early antiquity it was diplomatically correct for kings to take extravagant gifts to other kings, whether infant or grown, when they visited them for whatever reason.

We have texts from the city of Mari related to the Ancient Near East from as far back as 1850 BC that record the vast inventories of gifts that were exchanged between kings of greater or lesser degrees when they were meeting each other. These texts reveal that prodigious quantities of gold, ebony, ivory, lapis lazuli, garments, and sweet oil would be sent in each direction as part of diplomatic protocol. But even though these gifts added up to incredible sums, they pale in comparison to first millennium BC practices.

Osorkon (889 BC) gave gifts to Egypt in the form of vessels, statues, furnishings, and the like that totaled 445 metric tons of gold. The Queen of Sheba took an extraordinary abundance of gifts to the court of Solomon. However, the record tells us that her breath was taken away at the grandeur of Solomon's obvious wealth.

Jesus' little band received so much that they needed a treasurer (namely Judas). It was at the Cross that Jesus "became poor."

There is an abundance of records detailing what was considered diplomatically appropriate in the quantities of gift giving. In fact, if a king's level of wealth was not represented in his gift or if the stature of the receiving king were not sufficiently reflected, the receiving king would let the giver know in no uncertain terms that he had been slighted by the meanness of the gift.

The number of the magi who went to see Jesus was not limited necessarily to just three. This is often assumed just because three categories of gifts are mentioned in Scripture. There were probably many magi. And the gifts they took were not just three single items of gold, frankincense, and myrrh; rather, these are the headings of inventories that would each have included many different items. This was the normal practice for recording indexes of gifts for kings.

We can surmise that the wealth and influence of the magi was clearly considerable from the impact their coming had upon Herod. These gifts set Jesus up for life. The gifts were for Him personally, not His family (although it would be reasonable to suggest that once Jesus understood what His wealth was, He would have shared it with His earthly family).

During His ministry Jesus was provided for by wealthy women who followed Him as He traveled.

> ...and Joanna the wife of Chuza, Herod's steward, and Susanna, and many others who provided for Him from their substance.
>
> LUKE 8:3

These were wealthy people and there were many of them. They provided for all of the Messiah's material needs. In fact, Jesus' little band received so much that they needed a treasurer (namely Judas). It was at the Cross that Jesus "became poor."

Paul managed to travel three times around the Roman Empire, had enough money to pay for a Roman trial, and was kept in prison for two years by the Roman procurator of Judea, Felix. The sole reason for Paul's captivity was that Felix hoped for a bribe from the apostle. Felix would not have held Paul captive for so long for just a small amount. He knew Paul could deliver a substantial sum, and he was waiting for that (Acts 24:26).

If we are not meant to prosper, then it is only logical to conclude that God wants us to be poor and to fail in life so that we don't succeed and become prosperous.

Paul told Philemon to charge to his account anything the runaway slave Onesimus owed him. This might have been any amount, yet Paul was confident that he could cover it, no matter how much it was. The apostle was able to support an entire ministry team that traveled the world with him. As he labored at his craft, he prospered because of the blessing God had placed on his life (Acts 20:34).

Paul, being a strict Pharisee, would have observed tithing as a regular practice all his life. He preached on abundant giving and also on laying aside the firstfruits of a person's prosperity at the beginning of each week. He fully accepted that Christians would prosper.

> *On the first **day** of the week let each one of you lay something aside, storing up as he may prosper.*
>
> 1 CORINTHIANS 16:2

God's will is that we enjoy abundance in our lives so that we are able to assist others.

Those people who believe that Christians should not prosper ought to become seriously committed to being poor. If we are not meant to prosper, then it is only logical to conclude that God wants us to be poor and to fail in life so that we don't succeed and become prosperous. That would mean that He does not want us to do well in life, that He does not want us to be blessed with good things, with an abundance for our lives and those of others.

If God wants His children to be poor (while He himself lives in the vast abundance and glories of heaven), then we certainly should not be living in countries where the government will look after us in our poverty. We should be off to India, where we would mark out a piece of pavement for our home or live in a cardboard box. And we certainly should not seek wealth for medical needs or food. We should be scraping around rubbish tins looking for scraps of food along with the rest of the poor. That is what it is to be poor. If it is the will of God for us to be poor, then should we not do it with all our might? Should we not become as poor as the poorest?

At this point most will be saying, "Don't be ridiculous. We're not talking about that kind of poor. We should have just enough to get by moderately."

How much is "just enough to get by"? And for whom to get by? You! That has to be about the most selfish kind of Christianity ever postulated. How are you going to pay your neighbor's rent when he is out of work? How will you be able to pick up a person who has been run over, robbed, beaten, and left half dead on the side of the road?

How will you be able to take him to the hospital and then tell them you'll pay whatever it takes to get him healed?

Jesus said a true believer is someone who pays the price for the healing of people who are wounded (Luke 10:33). And this is not talking about spiritual healing. James says that mere religious talk is futile (James 2:16). Real religion is when we physically help people. This is impossible if we don't have the means to do it. God's will is that we enjoy abundance in our lives so that we are able to assist others.

> *Paul goes on to declare that abundance is decreed for our lives so that we can engage in every good work.*

*And God **is** able to make all grace abound toward you, that you, always having all sufficiency in all **things,** may have an abundance for every good work.*

2 Corinthians 9:8

This is one of the largest and most wonderful scriptures in the Bible. It says that God will cause an abundance to come into our lives because of his grace toward us. Even though we don't deserve grace, even though we have done nothing to merit His favor, He has chosen to place His grace and favor on our lives and it manifests in abundance.

This is the will of God—that we enjoy an abundance not just on payday, not just when the tax refund comes through, not just when we get a bonus, not just when we receive an inheritance, but always. That means every single day of our lives. God desires that we enjoy complete sufficiency in all things such that there is not one area in which we are insufficient.

Obedience to the law meant incredible blessing, but disobedience brought astonishing judgment.

But there's more! Paul goes on to declare that abundance is decreed for our lives so that we can engage in every good work. We might think we're just going to get involved in giving to one missionary, or supporting a particular ministry, or giving to just one or two people who have needs. But the Lord wants us to have such abundance that we can be a blessing to every good work. This is what the church is meant to be.

There is meant to be such prosperity in the church that we are able to give to all the needs of those around us all the time, in abundance.

If Jesus died to remove the curse,
then that is what has happened.
The curse has been removed.

6

The Curse of the Law and Its Demise

*Christ has redeemed us from the curse of the law, having become a curse for us (for it is written, **"Cursed is everyone who hangs on a tree"**), that the blessing of Abraham might come upon the Gentiles in Christ Jesus, that we might receive the promise of the Spirit through faith.*

GALATIANS 3:13-14

Paul actually declares that there is not a single blessing available that we haven't received.

Blessed be the God and Father of our Lord Jesus Christ, who has blessed us with every spiritual blessing in the heavenly places in Christ.

EPHESIANS 1:3

But because Christ has sacrificed His life to remove the curse, we are blessed with more than enough.

The curse of the law, outlined in Leviticus 26 and Deuteronomy 28, makes for hair-raising reading. Obedience to the law meant incredible blessing, but disobedience brought astonishing judgment. The terrible thing about the law is that it was impossible to keep (according to Paul); therefore, the curses outlined in these two passages are inevitable for those who do not know the Lord. The curse brought terrible catastrophes upon the circumstances of those affected. The death of Jesus was to disarm the power of these curses.

"But it shall come to pass, if you do not obey the voice of the LORD your God, to observe carefully all His commandments and His statutes which I command you today, that all these curses will come upon you and over-take you:

"Cursed **shall** you **be** in the city, and cursed **shall** you **be** in the country."

DEUTERONOMY 28:15-16

This meant that life in the city would be cursed: the marketplace, the entertainment world, the justice systems, the education system, the hospitals, the religious establishments, the transport and communications networks, the media, the sporting world, the industries, the finances, the banking systems, the housing—all the circumstances of the city would be cursed. Likewise in the countryside: all the grain crops, the dairy produce, the animal farms, the rivers, the rainfall, the seed for planting, the harvesting, the weather, the health of the crops and the animals—all would come under the curse.

*"Cursed **shall** be your basket and your kneading bowl."*

DEUTERONOMY 28:17

Whatever was taken from the field for preparation in the house would be either not enough or of poor quality. The kneading bowl would not bring enough dough for cooking to satisfy the family. The preparation of food would be insufficient, or else the food would taste terrible and have little nourishment. But because Christ has sacrificed His life to remove the curse, we are blessed with more than enough. All the food is blessed—it tastes great and there is an abundance of it.

*"Cursed **shall be** the fruit of your body and the produce of your land, the increase of your cattle and the offspring of your flocks."*

DEUTERONOMY 28:18

When you receive Christ, the good news is that the curse is removed.

Under the curse your sons and daughters would bring you trouble and difficulty. They would be a curse to you instead of a blessing. That is if you even managed to have children, because the curse would come on the womb and render it barren. Even the produce of the land would not reproduce. It would fail to give you seed to sow for next year's crop. Your cattle and sheep would not reproduce. They would be barren, and whatever they might bring forth would be so inferior that it would be useless for selling or even for using on the farm.

Christ died to remove these curses. Our sons and daughters will be a blessing to us. Infertile couples will bear children. There will not only be enough; there will be an abundance beyond what we need. There will not be just a maintaining of what already exists, but there will be an unending increase of the blessing upon people's lives, all because of the work of the Cross.

*"Cursed **shall** you **be** when you come in, and cursed **shall** you **be** when you go out."*

DEUTERONOMY 28:19

Under the curse, when you came into the house things would go wrong and your homecoming would not be pleasant. Your house would not be a refuge. It would be a place you would want to get away from. Even when you went out, things would go wrong. The car would break down. Accidents would happen. You might have planned a good time, but it would turn out miserable because it wouldn't go as you'd hoped it would. Everything would be miserable. You would receive fines for parking in the wrong spot or for speeding. People would steal things from you. You would wish you hadn't gone out at all.

When you receive Christ, the good news is that the curse is removed. Coming home is beautiful. Your home is a refuge. Your car runs well. When you go out you have a good time. Protection covers your home and your belongings. Even if things do go wrong, they will be forced to turn around for good because there is no curse on you. Instead you carry the blessing of God.

> "The LORD will send on you cursing, confusion, and rebuke in all that you set your hand to do, until you are destroyed and until you perish quickly, because of the wickedness of your doings in which you have forsaken Me."
>
> DEUTERONOMY 28:20

Christ absorbed the curse in His body, and through His death He annihilated all the terrible plagues identified here.

Under the curse you would be confused and not know what to do. You would seek guidance and get none. You would try to make decisions but never feel confident. You would attempt to start a business and, although all the statistics might have said it would go well, it would not succeed because of the curse and God's rebuke upon all that you set your hand to.

But because the curse has been removed through Christ's death, all confusion is also removed. You are set free to make clear-minded decisions. Even a little effort is rewarded in a big way. Because blessing rests on you, you make strong decisions that work well for you.

> "The LORD will make the plague cling to you until He has consumed you from the land which you are going to possess. The LORD will strike you with consumption, with fever, with inflammation, with severe burning fever, with the sword, with scorching, and with mildew; they shall pursue you until you perish."
>
> DEUTERONOMY 28:21-22

Under the curse physical sicknesses would cling to you and not go away. They would cling to you even though you might take all kinds of medication. Some of the afflictions that would cling to you include "consumption" (this has been identified as pulmonary tuberculosis–phthisis, or as the side effects of wasting and emaciation from prolonged bouts of malarial fever, or perhaps even cancer); "fever" (referring to any number of diseases, including malaria, typhoid, typhus, dysentery, chronic diarrhea or cholera); "inflammation" (when the healing processes of the body fail and an injury gets worse rather than better or becomes infected); "the sword" (that is, being struck by the sword and wounded by the effects of war); and "scorching and mildew" (referring to drought and diseases that would come upon the crops of Israel so that they would fail to come to fruit). Because of the curse of the law, all these sicknesses and afflictions would follow after the Israelites until they would perish.

Christ absorbed the curse in His body, and through His death He annihilated all the terrible plagues identified here. Neither sickness, nor war, nor plagues upon people and crops will fall on you. Others may get sick with these diseases, but you will avoid them. These illnesses will not rest on you because you are under the blessing, not the curse.

*"And your heavens which **are** over your head shall be bronze, and the earth which is under you **shall be** iron.*

Under the

blessing things

are different.

The LORD will change the rain of your land to powder and dust; from the heaven it shall come down on you until you are destroyed."

DEUTERONOMY 28:23-24

Under the curse, drought would ravage the land so that the earth would become as hard as iron, and dust rather than rain would cover the sky until destruction came. But when a nation embraces Christ as its Savior, the curse is broken and the blessing of God overtakes all the curses, breaking the worst of conditions (in this case, an agricultural community, the worst thing being drought).

*"The LORD will cause you to be defeated before your enemies; you shall go out one way against them and flee seven ways before them; and you shall become troublesome to all the kingdoms of the earth. Your carcasses shall be food for all the birds of the air and the beasts of the earth, and no one shall frighten **them** away."*

DEUTERONOMY 28:25-26

Under the curse, instead of defeating your enemies, they would defeat you. Note that the Word says you will have enemies. Under the blessing, however, you triumph over them. Under the curse, you would flee from your opposition. You would not enjoy the favor of other nations; rather, you would be a nuisance to the nations of the earth and the people of the earth would be happy to see you destroyed by the birds and beasts.

Under the blessing things are different. It is important for the church to accept that it is the light of this world, that it holds the answer. Too often the church has been considered a nuisance and perceived as having no value.

> *"The LORD will strike you with the boils of Egypt, with tumours, with the scab, and with the itch, from which you cannot be healed. The LORD will strike you with madness and blindness and confusion of heart."*
>
> DEUTERONOMY 28:27-28

Under the curse, the sicknesses of the world would come upon you: "boils" (a general biblical term refer-ring to inflamed swellings of the skin—the Hebrew word literally means ulcers; "tumors" (a disease most commentators find difficult to identify but generally agree is fatal); "the scab" and "the itch" (referring to skin diseases such as eczema, leprosy, scales, and ringworm). Incurable diseases

As the curse is removed, we are released from things that bind us and are set free from oppressors.

were predicted to be part of the curse. Insanity, blindness, and confusion would also come upon those who were under the curse of the law.

With the curse removed, however, the sicknesses of the world have no access into our lives. Through the blessing of God we will enjoy good health and receive healing of any illness that may occur. We will be blessed with sanity, vision, and peace in our hearts.

> *"And you shall grope at noonday, as a blind man gropes in darkness; you shall not prosper in your ways; you shall be only oppressed and plundered continually, and no one shall save **you**."*
>
> DEUTERONOMY 28:29

Under the curse oppressors and those who would wish to take advantage of you would overcome you. You would be "ripped off" again and again and wonder why. The curse of the law rests upon the person who has not received Christ. Under these conditions no one seeks to help the unfortunate out of their plight. No one would come to their aid.

As the curse is removed, we are released from things that bind us and are set free from oppressors. Rather than people taking advantage of us, we are blessed with great business deals, enormous bargains, and incredible bonuses. If we do happen to find ourselves in difficulty, people will come to our aid and help us to find a way out of the problem.

> *"You shall betroth a wife, but another man shall lie with her; you shall build a house, but you shall not dwell in it; you shall plant a vineyard, but shall not gather its grapes. Your ox **shall be** slaughtered before your eyes, but you shall not eat of it; your donkey **shall be** violently taken away from before you, and shall not be restored you; your sheep **shall be** given to your enemies, and you shall have no one to rescue **them.** Your sons and your daughters **shall be** given to another people, and your eyes shall look and fail*
> *with longing for them all day long; and **there shall be** no strength in your hand. A nation whom you have not known shall eat the fruit of your land and the produce of your labour, and you shall be only oppressed and crushed continually. So you shall be driven mad because of the sight which your eyes see."*

DEUTERONOMY 28:30-34

The blessing of God means your spouse will remain faithful, the home and business you build will be blessed, and you and your family will enjoy the fruit of your labor.

Under the curse all sense of security would depart from you. Another person would sleep with your wife. You

> Maybe the greatest blessing we can know is the presence of God in our lives.

would build your own home but not live in it. For one reason or another someone else would live in the house you thought you were building for yourself. You would start a business but someone else would buy it out and reap all the benefits. This is the curse of the law.

You would work hard to obtain and create something, but others would reap the benefits. All your inventions, hard work, and efforts would reap nothing because others would take away your employees, your management team, your workers, and your clients—all would be taken from you.

Your children would depart from you and your heart would break over longing for them, yet you would have no ability to win them back. Strangers—not even family or friends—would consume and enjoy the fruit of all your hard work. All these conditions would produce instability of mind as a kind of madness sets in.

Free from the curse because of the death of Jesus Christ, the blessing of God means your spouse will remain faithful, the home and business you build will be blessed, and you and your family will enjoy the fruit of your labor. Clients, employees, and family members will be loyal to you. You will enjoy great peace of mind as you and your family and friends enjoy the blessing of heaven.

> *"The LORD will strike you in the knees and on the legs with severe boils which cannot be healed, and from the sole of your foot to the top of your head."*
>
> DEUTERONOMY 28:35

Under the blessing of God, the people of God find respect and are often feared.

These sound like the kinds of boils that Job had (Job 2:7). They have been identified with smallpox or with a parasitic infection called treponematosis.

> *"The LORD will bring you and the king whom you set over you to a nation which neither you nor your fathers have known, and there you shall serve other gods—wood and stone."*
>
> DEUTERONOMY 28:36

The worst effect of these curses is that the glory of God would no longer be among you, but rather lifeless gods of mere wood and stone that give no glory at all to those who serve them. You would be transported out of the kingdom of God into a strange land, where you would have no friends, only strangers.

Maybe the greatest blessing we can know, being set free from the curse, is the presence of God in our lives—at home, at work, in the car, on holiday, in family life, and in solitary life. God is with us. This is the greatest blessing of the New Testament. This is the reason Jesus suffered such a torturous death—to connect us with His Father and to enable us to remain in fellowship with Him.

> *"And you shall become an astonishment, a proverb, and a byword among all nations where the LORD will drive you."*
>
> DEUTERONOMY 28:37

Freedom from the curse guarantees that your seed will produce the maximum possible, your harvest will come in and your business will grow.

Under the curse, respect is lost and is replaced by mockery. You would be sent to lands where the inhabitants would hate you. People would make fun of you and joke about you. Under the blessing of God the people of God find respect and are often feared. Godly people become the most prosperous and exercise influential leadership through natural and supernatural means. Their words come to pass and they express practical compassion that ensures they are valued above all others in the community. The action of servanthood makes them indispensable, and the acts of God that accompany them guarantee they are reverenced.

> *"You shall carry much seed out to the field but gather little in, for the locust shall consume it. You shall plant vineyards and tend **them**, but you shall neither drink of the wine nor gather the **grapes;** for the worms shall eat them. You shall have olive trees throughout all your territory, but you shall not anoint **yourself** with the oil; for your olives shall drop off. You shall beget sons and daughters, but they shall not be yours; for they shall go into captivity. Locusts shall consume all your trees and the produce of your land."*

DEUTERONOMY 28:38-42

Under the curse, all your efforts to produce crops, build businesses, plant orchards, and raise stock would fail because diseases and insects would destroy them. Even your sons and daughters would be a source of grief to you because strangers would steal them away into slavery and captivity.

Freedom from the curse guarantees that your seed will produce the maximum possible, your harvest will come in, and your business will grow.

The blessing of God brings the power of influence, so that the people of God are able to change society.

Your stock will increase. Your sons and daughters will be a blessing to you and not a burden. You will not be weighed down by debt, reducing your capacity to enjoy life. The blessing on you will accelerate your earning ability, increase your business, and maximize your results.

> *"The alien who **is** among you shall rise higher and higher above you, and you shall come down lower and lower. He shall lend to you, but you shall not lend to him; he shall be the head, and you shall be the tail."*
>
> DEUTERONOMY 28:43-44

Under the curse, strangers and foreigners in your land would rise up to rule over you in areas such as civic government, finance, business, entertainment, sports, and education, so that you would be servile to them. They would lend you money, and they would be the "head" while you would be "wagged" like the tail. But because you have received Christ and because His work on the Cross is effective in obliterating the curse of the law, you will rise higher and higher. The power of "lift" will be in you.

Under the blessing of God, the curses are gradually lifted off us until none are left. We serve the Lord with joy and gladness of heart.

Instead of your seeking money from the world, the world will seek money from you. You will gain control and the power of direction by being the head and not the tail.

The blessing of God brings the power of influence, so that the people of God are able to change society. They gain power through financial abundance or by being elevated to positions of power. Under the curse, we lose the ability to be effective, but under the blessing, effectiveness becomes a gift from God.

> "Moreover all these curses shall come upon you and pursue and overtake you, until you are destroyed, because you did not obey the voice of the LORD your God, to keep His commandments and His statutes which He commanded you. And they shall be upon you for a sign and a wonder, and on your descendants forever.
>
> "Because you did not serve the LORD your God with joy and gladness of heart, for the abundance of everything, therefore you shall serve your enemies, whom the LORD will send against you, in hunger, in thirst, in nakedness, and in need of everything; and He will put a yoke of iron on your neck until He has destroyed you."
>
> DEUTERONOMY 28:45-48

Because of your disobedience to the Lord these curses would eventually overwhelm and destroy you. You would become enslaved to foreigners, living in abject poverty, in need of everything.

Under the blessing of God the curses are gradually lifted off us until none are left. We serve the Lord with joy and gladness of heart. Instead of hunger and thirst and nakedness, we are filled with good food and drink and we are the best dressed. We are in need of nothing.

Under the blessing, however, you cannot be overwhelmed by enemies.

"The LORD will bring a nation against you from afar, from the end of the earth, as swift as the eagle flies, a nation whose language you will not understand, a nation of fierce countenance, which does not respect the elderly nor show favor to the young. And they shall eat the increase of your livestock and the produce of your land, until you are destroyed; they shall not leave you grain or new wine or oil, or the increase of your cattle or the offspring of your flocks, until they have destroyed you.

"They shall besiege you at all your gates until your high and fortified walls, in which you trust, come down throughout all your land; and they shall besiege you at all your gates throughout all your land which the LORD your God has given you. You shall eat the fruit of your own body, the flesh of your sons and your daughters whom the LORD your God has given you, in the siege and desperate straits in which your enemy shall distress you.

"The sensitive and very refined man among you will be hostile toward his brother, toward the wife of his bosom, and toward the rest of his children whom he leaves behind, so that he will not give any of them the flesh of his children whom he will eat, because he has nothing left in the siege and desperate straits in which your enemy shall distress you at all your gates.

"The tender and delicate woman among you, who would not venture to set the sole of her foot on the ground because of her delicateness and sensitivity, will refuse to the husband of her bosom, and to her son and her daughter, her placenta which comes out from between her feet and her children whom she bears; for she will eat them secretly for lack of everything in the siege and desperate straits in which your enemy shall distress you at all your gates."

DEUTERONOMY 28:49-57

Because of the curse, merciless and fierce enemies would come against you and completely destroy you. They would besiege you to the point where you would be debased to do terrible things, even to your own family, such as destroying your own children.

Under the blessing, however, you cannot be overwhelmed by enemies. Should an enemy attack you, they will not win. Your cities, houses, and families will be secure. Your children will grow up and develop to their full potential, blessed in every way.

Set free from the curse, God's only joy is to see you happy, blessed, and living in victory.

"If you do not carefully observe all the words of this law that are written in this book, that you may fear this glorious and awesome name, THE LORD YOUR GOD, then the LORD will bring upon you and your descendants extraordinary plagues—great and prolonged plagues—and serious and prolonged sicknesses."

DEUTERONOMY 28:58-59

Plagues that have never even been heard of would come upon those who have this curse upon them. They would last for extraordinarily long times, be uncommonly large, and of such an unusual nature that there would be no cure for them. But under the blessing of God, you will be set free from plagues that are attacking everyone else. If you do get sick it will not last long. You will get over illness quickly.

*"Moreover He will bring back on you all the diseases of Egypt, of which you were afraid, and they shall cling to you. Also every sickness and every plague, which **is** not written in this Book of the Law, will the LORD bring upon you until you are destroyed. You shall be left few in number, whereas you were as the stars of heaven in multitude, because you would not obey the voice of the LORD your God."*

DEUTERONOMY 28:60-62

Under the curse, rather than being a vast multitude you would become pathetically few in number. Your power, nobility, and strength among others would be reduced to nothing. But because we are set free from the curse, the church will increase more and more throughout the earth. Under the blessing we will outstrip the numbers of people in the world who are not saved.

> "And it shall be, **that** just as the LORD rejoiced over you to do you good and multiply you, so the LORD will rejoice over you to destroy you and bring you to nothing; and you shall be plucked from off the land which you go to possess."
>
> DEUTERONOMY 28:63

Under the curse God would be happy to destroy you because you were such an offense and grief to Him. He would cause you to be removed from your homeland where all your fond memories, family relationships, and possessions were. You would be sent to a land where you have no history or sense of belonging.

Set free from the curse, God's only joy is to see you happy, blessed, and living in victory. His great joy is to multiply you and do you good. His determination is that you dwell safely in the land.

Free from the curse you will be secure, safe, and restful, not restless.

For a curse to be effective, it must have grounds for resting on a person's life.

"*Then the L*ORD *will scatter you among all peoples, from one end of the earth to the other, and there you shall serve other gods, which neither you nor your fathers have known—wood and stone. And among those nations you shall find no rest, nor shall the sole of your foot have a resting place; but there the L*ORD *will give you a trembling heart, failing eyes, and anguish of soul. Your life shall hang in doubt before you; you shall fear day and night, and have no assurance of life. In the morning you shall say, 'Oh, that it were evening!' And at evening you shall say, 'Oh, that it were morning!' because of the fear which terrifies your heart, and because of the sight which your eyes see.*"

DEUTERONOMY 28:64-67

Under the curse, you would experience restlessness and anxiety. You would never enjoy security, stability, or peacefulness. Your heart would be anxious and panic-stricken, as you would have no vision for the future. Your soul would be in pain and anguish. You would have doubts about whether or not you were going to live, and you would never feel safe about your well-being. You would wish your life would end, that your days would be over quickly, so that you would no longer experience the terror and fear in your life.

Free from the curse you will be secure, safe, and restful, not restless. Your life will not be in doubt; rather, you will be completely assured of the blessing. Instead of fear filling your heart, faith will overwhelm all your doubts. The vision you have of the future will cause you to be inspired and enthused with fresh energy.

> "And the LORD will take you back to Egypt in ships, by the way of which I said to you, 'You shall never see it again.' And there you shall be offered for sale to your enemies as male and female slaves, but no one will buy **you**."
>
> DEUTERONOMY 28:68

Under the curse you would be taken back to places you never wanted to return to. Your whole life would seem to go backwards. You would try at least to eke out a living, but no one would want you or employ you. The final and most terrible thing would be that you would be rejected and not wanted by anybody.

Under the blessing of God you progress, you move forward. You will be the one calling the shots. If Jesus has died to remove the curse, then that is what has happened—the curse has been removed. For a curse to be effective, it must have grounds for resting on a person's life. But once the blood of Christ has washed all sins from our souls, there remains no ground for any curse whatsoever to gain access to our lives.

Like a flitting sparrow, like a flying swallow,
So a curse without cause shall not alight.

PROVERBS 26:2

This means that all these curses have been removed and reversed. Under the blessing of God, instead of curses, blessings shower down on our lives in all those areas that were previously cursed under the law. It means our life in the city is blessed—the marketplace, the entertainment world, the justice systems, the world of education, hospitals, the religious establishments, transport and communications systems, the media, the sporting world, industries, the banking systems, housing—all the circumstances of the city will be blessed. Likewise in the countryside—all of the grain crops, the dairy produce, the animal farms, the rivers, the rainfall, the seed for planting, the harvesting, the weather, the health of the crops and the animals—all would come under the blessing of God.

Whatever is taken from the field for preparation in the house will be more than enough and of the very best quality. Food preparation will be abundant and the food will taste fantastic and be super-nourishing.

Your sons and daughters will bring ease and joy. They will be a blessing to you instead of a curse. You will have beautiful children. You will not be barren because blessing will rest on the womb and render it fruitful.

Even the produce of the land will multiply with abundance. There will be a full supply of seed to sow for next year's crop.

Your cattle and sheep will reproduce—they will not be barren. And what they bring forth will be superior to anything your competition can produce.

When you come into your house, things will go well. Homecoming will be a joyful occasion. Your house will be a refuge. It will be your castle to retreat to from the pressures of the world.

When you step out of your home, things will work well for you. The car will run well. Accidents will be avoided. If there does happen to be a breakdown or an accident, it will work out for good.

Your plans will come to fruition. You will not be besieged by troubles and your goods will be safe from thieves.

You will always know exactly what to do. You will seek guidance and be clear about your direction. You will make decisions and feel confident about them.

You will start a business and it will do well because of the blessing of God upon all that you set your hand to.

> God Himself will be happy to bless you because you are such a blessing to Him.

Physical health will rest upon you. Any sicknesses or wounds that you do happen to incur will heal swiftly. Any medical procedures will be completely successful.

Rain will drench the land so that the earth becomes soft.

Instead of being defeated by your enemies, you will defeat them. Under the blessing your enemies will flee from you. You will be favored by the nations. The people of the earth will be happy to see you blessed.

Incurable disease will disappear from you. Healing will come from God.

You will overcome oppressors and those who might wish to take advantage of you. When you are in trouble people will come to your aid and give you help.

With the blessing of God you will have great security. Your marriage will be secure. You will enjoy living in the home you build. You will reap the benefits of the business you build. In fact, under the blessing of God you will reap where others have labored. You will benefit from those who thought to harm you. You children will inherit your wealth. You will see your children grow in God and in good health. You will bless others—friends, families and strangers. You will enjoy great peace of mind and sanity from living a secure life free from anxiety.

The glory of God will manifest among you. You will worship and delight in God. You will be planted in the kingdom of God with many friends, good support, leaders, and a future.

People will come to you for guidance and coaching. They will look to you for leadership. They will use you as an example for living.

Strangers will not rule over you, but rather you will be able to guide and bless them because of the blessing of God upon you.

You will multiply in number and become a vast multitude.

Your power, nobility, and strength amongst others will increase.

God himself will be happy to bless you because you are such a blessing to Him. He will cause you to be established in your homeland, where all your fond memories, family relationships, and possessions are.

We are counted as righteous, just like Jesus, because His life has been freely credited to our account.

You will experience rest, security, stability, and peacefulness. Your heart will be calm and full of faith, with vision for the future. Your soul will experience joy and health. You would be full of faith about your future.

You will be taken to places you always wanted to go. Your whole life will move forward. People everywhere will seek you out to be your friend, to be connected to you.

This is just the beginning of the great blessing of God.

For the law of the Spirit
of life in Christ Jesus
has made me free from
the law of sin and death.

Romans 8:2

7

Just Like Jesus

We must realize that Jesus did not live or die or rise from the dead for Himself. He did it all for us. His perfect life is imputed to us as righteousness (Jer. 23:6). We are counted as righteous, just like Jesus, because His life has been freely credited to our account. This is one of the most awesome facts about our salvation.

Jesus lived a perfect life. Scripture describes His life as being "without spot or blemish" (1 Pet. 1:19).

He was perfect in His relationship with God.

He was perfect in His relationships with other people—His family, community, and friends.

> We are declared righteous and perfect, not because we are in and of ourselves, but because Jesus is.

He was perfect in His moral life.

He was perfect in thought.

He was perfect in attitude.

He was perfect in motivation.

He was perfect in speech.

He was perfect in action.

He was perfect in obedience and calling.

He was perfect in pleasing the Father.

Jesus was sinless…without sin…without fault…perfect!

> God is not looking for ways to reject, condemn, and curse humanity. He has always been looking for ways to save us.

Jeremiah says in his writings that there will come a day when the Lord will be known as Jehovah-Tsidkenu, literally meaning "the Lord our righteousness" (Jer. 23:5-6). This is the kernel of our justification before God. We are declared righteous and perfect not because we are in and of ourselves, but because Jesus is. The Lord himself is our righteousness.

Let me explain how this works a little further. After the resurrection Jesus appears before the Father and presents His life. The Father views Jesus' life and declares it perfect. In fact, it is the very life God would have lived if He had become a human. And that is exactly the case.

> One of the most challenging obstacles we have to overcome in life is ourselves.

Jesus, being our advocate, explains to the Father that Phil Pringle down on planet earth desires to be right with Him, to enter heaven and to have a relationship with Him. The Father replies that this is out of the question, hopeless. He fully knows the life of Phil Pringle, and it falls far too short of the glory of God. It is full of faults and shortcomings, sins and iniquities. But Jesus says to the Father that He wants to "give" His perfect life to this human being so that he can be saved, acquitted of all guilt, and declared righteous before God in heaven. The Father agrees that this is a wonderful idea and accepts Jesus' act as legitimate.

God is not looking for ways to reject, condemn, and curse humanity. He has always been looking for ways to save us. This is the perfect way. It is a perfect salvation. The saved person places their trust in the righteousness of Christ, not their own. Then, in terms of righteousness,

> When we come to Christ, He doesn't offer us a new set of rules to live by.

they have exactly the same standing before God as Jesus himself has. They are placed in the position of being fully qualified to receive all the blessings that are promised to the righteous throughout Scripture.

This is "imputed" righteousness. This is salvation. It is the awesome gift of God. It is Jesus himself being given to our lives. We live by the righteousness of another—the righteousness of the perfect Jesus Christ. His life has been credited to our account. His death has removed all sin from our lives, and His resurrection has given us eternal life. He did it all for us, out of love for us. Love was His motive for doing all that He did.

One of the most challenging obstacles we have to overcome in life is ourselves. We are born with a nature that desires to sin. Our flesh has inherent impulses toward wrongdoing. We live in this fleshly nature until we are born again, at which point we have the option to become released from our self-nature and to embrace the nature of Christ.

Paul reveals that the sinful nature has been put to death in Christ.

*...knowing this, that our old man was crucified with **Him,** that the body of sin might be done away with, that we should no longer be slaves of sin.*

ROMANS 6:6

This nature is referred to in the Scripture as the "the old man," "the body of sin," "the old nature," and "the flesh." The impulses of this nature are referred to in various scriptures.

> God not only deals a deathblow to the sin impulse within us, but also to our love for sin.

But now you yourselves are to put off all these: anger, wrath, malice, blasphemy, filthy language out of your mouth. Do not lie to one another, since you have put off the old man with his deeds.

COLOSSIANS 3:8-9

Now the works of the flesh are evident, which are: adultery, fornication, uncleanness, lewdness, idolatry, sorcery, hatred, contentions, jealousies, outbursts of wrath, selfish ambitions, dissensions, heresies, envy, murders, drunkenness, revelries, and the like.

GALATIANS 5:19-21

The flesh is born with these inclinations in it. We have to teach children how to be good. It seems they need little instruction in the art of doing wrong! When we come to Christ, He doesn't offer us a new set of rules to live by. He offers a new spirit. This new life within us overwhelms the power of the flesh. The law of the Holy Spirit is a higher and more powerful law than the law of sin. Both are laws, but one is more powerful than the other.

> *For the law of the Spirit of life in Christ Jesus has made me free from the law of sin and death.*
>
> ROMANS 8:2

As we live in the Spirit for the Lord, the old nature is put to death.

It's like the law of aerodynamics. The law of gravity forces everything down to earth, but the laws of aerodynamics can actually overcome the downward pull of gravity and carry us up into the sky.

Ezekiel predicted this would happen.

> *"I will give you a new heart and put a new spirit within you; I will take the heart of stone out of your flesh and give you a heart of flesh. I will put My Spirit within you and cause you to walk in My statutes, and you will keep My judgments and do **them**."*
>
> EZEKIEL 36:26-27

Without this inward revolution, where the sin nature dies and the nature of righteousness is born, we are engaged in a continual internal war, struggling with the powerful negative woven into our self-nature.

God not only deals a deathblow to the sin impulse within us, but also to our love for sin. He gives us a new heart—a heart for God—with a desire for righteousness. This is an amazing thing.

One day we're in love with darkness; the next day we shun it in disgust. We suddenly love the light.

One day we're blaspheming the name of Jesus; the next day it's the dearest name under the sun to us.

One day we're cursing; the next day we're praying.

It happens in a moment. We are born again, and a new nature is deposited into our mortal frame.

Paul urges us to live in a zone where we take the initiative and "put on" the new nature while "putting off" the old (Eph. 4:22-24). We appropriate this reality by feeding the new nature and starving the old. As we live in the Spirit for the Lord, the old nature is put to death.

For if you live according to the flesh you will die; but if by the Spirit you put to death the deeds of the body, you will live.

Romans 8:13

I've heard it said that one of the punishments for murder in ancient Roman times was to chain the carcass of the victim to the back of the murderer. Eventually, the diseases from the decaying corpse would eat through into the healthy body of the criminal until he too died a slow, horrible death. This is a very vivid picture of what happens to the believer who fails to put off the "old nature." Eventually it will eat through into the new nature and bring death to it.

The death of the old nature involves a combination of effort from both the Christian and God. The starting point, however, is that Jesus has killed the self-nature in all of us through the Cross. The old Adamic nature is killed through the Cross, and a new species of being is created. Jesus is the new Adam, the first of a new race of people, void of the sinful streak that runs so deeply in Adam's line.

The trigger that releases this great work of the Cross is baptism. The word "baptism" literally means "to immerse into." The Christian is commanded to be baptized. We are to be "immersed into" a number of things.

1. The Holy Spirit (Matt. 3:11)

2. The Church (1 Cor. 12:13)

3. Water (Acts 2:38-41)

4. Fire (Matt. 3:11)

Note that we are immersed not sprinkled. This is an important point to grasp. Our death to the old is a total not partial dying, and our coming alive to the new is also a total coming alive.

> Or do you not know that as many of us as were baptized into Christ Jesus were baptized into His death? Therefore we were buried with Him through baptism into death, that just as Christ was raised from the dead by the glory of the Father, even so we also should walk in newness of life.
>
> For if we have been united together in the likeness of His death, certainly we also shall be **in the likeness** of **His** resurrection, knowing this, that our old man was crucified with **Him,** that the body of sin might be done away with, that we should no longer be slaves of sin.
>
> ROMANS 6:3-6

The Christian life demands a 100 percent commitment. It is impossible to live it any other way. Hence, we need to be baptized into (immersed in) the critical elements that enable us to live this most magnificent of lives.

It is useful at this point to cover a little history that underscores the importance of total immersion. The word "baptism" is an anglicized word. This means that when it was translated into English from the Greek, it was basically left as it was. There were reasons for this. The

King James Version of the Bible was commissioned by King James I of England. The King of England was also the recognized head of the Church of England. This responsibility had carried over from the days when the Church of England had broken away from the Church of Rome. When the pope had refused to grant King Henry VIII a divorce, Henry decided that he would nationalize the church in his country. Thus began the Church of England, the Anglican Church.

In the days of the early church people had been baptized by full immersion. However, as time had passed, for one reason or another, the practice of plunging new believers beneath the water passed away, as did the practice of baptizing a person only when they were of an age to understand the significance of what was happening. Instead, babies were baptized by sprinkling as a matter of standard religious practice if the parents were members of the church.

Neither did a person's spiritual state seem to matter—the ceremony was seen as enough in itself for entry into the church. In fact, the ceremony of baptism was considered to be the process by which a person became acceptable to God. In other words, a person was thought to become a Christian by virtue of infant baptism.

This has always been the danger of "religious acts." Too easily they degenerate into heartless, empty, lip-serving traditions. They are at best false securities; at worst, they are vigorous enemies of God and His work in people's hearts. So the practice of baptism became a ceremony of sprinkling with water for admission into the church.

Derek Prince tells us that the relationship between James I and his bishops was not always too cordial, and he did not wish the new translation of the Bible, published in his name and with his authority, to make his relationship with the bishops any worse. For this reason he allowed it to be understood that, as far as possible, nothing was to be introduced into the translation which would cause unnecessary offense to the bishops or which would be too obviously contrary to the practices of the established church. Hence the Greek word *baptize,* which could easily have become, in translation, a source of controversy, was never translated at all, but was simply written over into the English language.

> Noah's flood is symbolic of water baptism—the old generation perished in the water and the new generation was saved.

The Greek word *bapto* means "to whelm, to cover wholly with a fluid." It relates to washings and ablutions of all kinds. It is important that we understand the full meaning of this word because it relates to areas other than just water baptism, such as baptism in the Holy Spirit, baptism into Christ's body, and the baptism of suffering. None of these are a sprinkling experience. They all involve a complete immersion.

If we allow ourselves to think that baptism is a simply a sprinkling ceremony people participate in without any intelligent understanding of the event, we will dilute God's work in people's lives to a level of virtual nonexistence. Sadly, this is exactly the case in many Christian expressions.

In 1608 John Smyth baptized himself in Amsterdam. This was basically the beginning of the Baptist movement as we know it today. Smyth and his group recovered the vital truth of adult full immersion as a fulfillment of Christ's command to be baptized. Baptism, as practiced by Christians in the New Testament, has its roots in the Old Testament. Noah's flood is symbolic of water baptism— the old generation perished in the water and the new generation was saved. Thus began a whole new world.

*...the Divine longsuffering waited in the days of Noah, while **the** ark was being prepared, in which a few, that is,*

*eight souls, were saved through water.
There is also an antitype which now saves
us—baptism.*

1 PETER 3:20-21

Another picture of baptism involving deliverance from the old and
entering the new is Moses crossing the
Red Sea with three million Hebrews
behind him.

This is regarded
as an outward
expression of
an internal change
of heart.

*All our fathers were under the cloud,
all passed through the sea, all were
baptized into Moses in the cloud and in the sea.*

1 CORINTHIANS 10:1-2

These are two Old Testament pictures of baptism.
However, the practice of baptism actually has its begin-
nings in the Tabernacle of Moses. The priests were
required to cleanse themselves regularly in a large bowl
called the laver. It was positioned immediately after the
great bronze altar used for burnt sacrifices to God. The
laver itself was made from bronze mirrors donated by the
Israelite women. Parts of the sacrificed animals were also
washed in the laver. Thus the concept of cleansing by
water as part of approaching God was firmly in place.

Another historical event predating New Testament baptism is found in 2 Kings, chapter 5, in the story of an Assyrian commander called Naaman. Although a famous warrior with a powerful position in his nation, Naaman was also a leper. One of the foreign maids he had abducted from Israel advised him that there was help to be found in her country. She knew that the prophet Elisha could heal him.

The commander became convinced and made the journey to the prophet. Elisha instructed the man to dip himself seven times in the River Jordan to be healed. Although the proud general initially resisted Elisha's command, he eventually carried it out. The result—he was completely healed of leprosy. Leprosy is always seen as a symbol of sin in the Old Testament. And so Naaman is cleansed of his sin by immersing himself in the River Jordan.

The story of Naaman obviously sets the stage for John the Baptist, whom we find in the desert preaching a message of repentance to the Israelites. Those responding to his call must make a public profession that they are in fact leaving sin and turning to righteousness. The sign of their intent is that they are baptized, fully immersed as adults, in the River Jordan. This is regarded as an outward expression of an internal change of heart.

The Bible tells us that the whole region goes out to where John is preaching. He is experiencing a vast move of God. He knows his purpose, though: it is to prepare the way for another, his cousin Jesus. Jesus arrives in the midst of this revival and asks John to baptize Him too. Even though Christ had no sin, he said it was necessary to do this in order to "fulfill all righteousness."

> Baptism is God's means of identifying us with the death, burial, and resurrection of Jesus Christ.

After Christ has risen from the dead and the Holy Spirit has fallen on His followers, baptism loses none of its significance. It continues to be the recognized practice by which people publicly declare their commitment to repent and turn to God. Believers are quickly baptized after conversion.

Then those who gladly received his word were baptized.

ACTS 2:41

Not only does water baptism continue as an accepted practice of the church; it actually increases in importance to being an act that accompanies salvation.

"He who believes and is baptized will be saved; but he who does not believe will be condemned."

MARK 16.16

Baptism gains even further significance when Paul arrives on the scene and proclaims his revelation of the victory we gain through water baptism. As I have said earlier, not only are our sins forgiven when we are saved, but the person who commits the offenses—the sinner himself—is also blotted out. Simply plucking the fruit from a tree, no matter how sour it might be, doesn't prevent the tree from continuing to yield the same sour fruit. The tree itself must be killed.

The bias towards sin is in us from the day we are conceived.

Behold, I was brought forth in iniquity
And in sin my mother conceived me.

PSALM 51:5

Baptism in water is our life statement—not only that we are turning from sin, but that we are actually dying. We are declaring that the entire sum of our old life and the entire sum of our sin nature are now dead. We are also declaring that we are being resurrected into a totally new life in Christ.

Being lowered into the water of baptism is being crucified and buried with Christ. Being lifted up out of the water is being resurrected with Christ. Baptism is God's means of identifying us with the death, burial, and resurrection of Jesus Christ. Let's look at that awesome scripture again, awakening us to the fact that our old life has been actually crucified with Christ and that we are now a new creation in Christ.

> *Or do you not know that as many of us as were baptized into Christ Jesus were baptized into His death? Therefore we were buried with Him through baptism into death, that just as Christ was raised from the dead by the glory of the Father, even so we should walk in newness of life.*
>
> *For if we have been united together in the likeness of His death, certainly we also shall be in the likeness of His resurrection.*
>
> ROMANS 6:3-5

This is the ultimate experience of repentance—not just when sin dies, but when the sinner dies.

God is involved in the appropriation of this truth in a major way. The Christian life is not meant to be something we struggle and strive to live. It is to be as natural to us as breathing. If we find we are continually trying to be Christian, this truth needs to come alive in us.

Being a Christian is not something I have to think about or work hard at if I have been born again. I don't have to struggle to breathe or to digest food to be a human being. I am created for these things. It is exactly the same when it comes to being a Christian. We are created Christian when we come to Christ. Being comes before doing. I'm a human being before I'm a human doing.

As God takes us through various experiences in life, some will be painful. In such times the Lord can break us to His will so that we die to ourselves. Deep within each of us is a great shaft called "I" on which are all the levers of our lives. This "I" shaft is the motivator of all we do: when it turns, so do we.

All the levers move when "I" moves. What "I" wants to do, we do. However, there comes a day when God takes all our self-centeredness and self-will and puts it to death. He breaks it. Though it is a painful experience, this is one of the greatest days of victory we can ever enjoy. We die. We rest in peace.

This is the ultimate experience of repentance—not just when sin dies, but when the sinner dies. God removes the "I" shaft and replaces it with Christ. Now He, Jesus, becomes the deep motivator of our lives, of all our actions and attitudes. Now we are able to say along with Paul,

> *"I have been crucified with Christ; it is no longer I who live, but Christ lives in me."*
>
> GALATIANS 2:20

We are set free from ourselves through the great work of the Cross.

But God forbid that I should boast
except in the cross of
our Lord Jesus Christ,
by whom the world has
been crucified to me,
and I to the world.

Galatians 6:14

8

A World Away

Paul declares that because of the Cross the world is now dead to me and I am dead to the world. I am no longer under the domination of whatever is happening in the world because I have been transferred into the kingdom of God. In fact, Paul calls it a translation.

> *Who hath delivered us from the power of darkness, and hath **translated** us into the kingdom of his dear Son.*
>
> COLOSSIANS 1:13 KJV (italics mine)

Enoch was translated from his earthly life so that he didn't experience death (Heb. 11:5). The Bible says he could not be found because God had "taken" him. In much the same way Philip the evangelist was "caught away" from the Gaza Strip road to a town called Azotus (Acts 8:39). He disappeared right in front of the Ethiopian whom he had just baptized and immediately reappeared at a town about 30 kilometers away. This was a supernatural "translation."

We too have been supernaturally "caught away" from one place and landed in another. We have been "translated" from the kingdom of darkness to the kingdom of light. We are no longer under the dominion of the darkness of this world, but rather we are now dominated by light.

The word "power" in the verse above is translated from the Greek word *exousia,* which means "privilege," or "authority" (i.e. force, capacity, competency, freedom, mastery, magistrate, superhuman, potentate, token of control, delegated influence, jurisdiction, liberty, power, right and/or strength). Whatever controls the world no longer controls us. The spirit that is at work in the people of the world no longer holds any power over our lives.

This is seen graphically in various places in Scripture. When Moses was seeking to bring the children of Israel out of bondage in Egypt, God rained down judgments on Egypt time and again. But the people of God and their families, their land, their businesses, and their possessions were unaffected.

The Israelites lived in the Land of Goshen, a choice area that had been gifted to them due to the favor on Joseph's life. The Pharaoh of Joseph's day had benefited so much from Joseph's guidance, wisdom, and oversight that he rewarded him by giving his family some of the best land in Egypt. We are told that when the curses from God fell on the land in Moses' time, Goshen was spared.

We live in Christ not in the world.

> *"But the LORD will make a distinction between the livestock of Israel and that of Egypt, so that no animal belonging to the Israelites will die."*
>
> EXODUS 9:4 NIV

> *And the next day the LORD did it: All the livestock of the Egyptians died, but not one animal belonging to the Israelites died.*
>
> EXODUS 9:6 NIV

> *The only place it did not hail was the land of Goshen, where the Israelites were.*
>
> EXODUS 9:26 NIV

> *No one could see anyone else or leave his place for three days. Yet all the Israelites had light in the places where they lived.*
>
> EXODUS 10:23 NIV

"There will be loud wailing throughout Egypt—worse than there has ever been or ever will be again. But among the Israelites not a dog will bark at any man or animal. Then you will know that the LORD makes a distinction between Egypt and Israel."

EXODUS 11:6-7 NIV

"The blood will be a sign for you on the houses where you are; and when I see the blood, I will pass over you. No destructive plague will touch you when I strike Egypt."

EXODUS 12:13 NIV

The dreadful finale of these judgments was the death of all the firstborn children throughout the land. Every Israelite household was told to paint the blood of a slain lamb over the doorposts of their home. The angel of death who brought the plague of death to Egypt passed over the homes of God's people. Through the blood of a slain lamb, each household was set free from the world and all the terror of its judgments.

In Genesis 26 we are told that Isaac remained in the Land of Canaan, even though there was a famine in the land. He stayed because God told him to. He was to remain in the Promised Land. For us this represents remaining in Christ. Just as the Israelites remained in Goshen in Egypt and avoided the plagues, as we remain in

Christ we are free from the curses that
the world endures.

We live in Christ not, in the world.
We live in the ways of Christ, not the
ways of the world. We become successful by honest means, not by cheating.
We live like Christ, not like the world.
We live separated to God, separate from
the world.

> Whatever calamity
> might come on the
> world, we are able
> to escape it through
> being in Christ.

The devil would love us to compro-
mise this position. He tries to seduce us away from the
principles of living in Christ by having us believe that
going the way of the world is the sure way to succeed. But
when we sacrifice our integrity to the god of success, we
move out of Christ. This is what Isaac was tempted to
do—to go down to Egypt when things got tough. But he
was warned to remain in Canaan. As he obeyed, blessing
came on his world.

> *There was a famine in the land, besides the first famine
> that was in the days of Abraham. And Isaac went to
> Abimelech king of the Philistines, in Gerar. Then the* LORD
> *appeared to him and said: "Do not go down to Egypt; live
> in the land of which I shall tell you. Dwell in this land, and
> I will be with you and bless you; for to you and your*

> *descendants I give all these lands, and I will perform the oath which I swore to Abraham your father."*
>
> GENESIS 26:1-3

God does wonders among His people that no other group on earth experience.

Isaac simply carried on his normal farming activities, and while the rest of the land was in famine he prospered enormously. While all the fields around him were brown and barren, his were green and flourishing. All around him people were losing, but he was winning.

> *Then Isaac sowed in that land, and reaped in the same year a hundredfold; and the LORD blessed him. The man began to prosper, and continued prospering until he became very prosperous; for he had possessions of flocks and possessions of herds and a great number of servants. So the Philistines envied him.*
>
> GENESIS 26:12-14

Noah's ark is another very clear picture of God's people being set free from the world. Whatever calamity might come on the world, we are able to escape it through being in Christ. All those who believed God and got into the ark were saved from the terrible disaster that covered the earth. It seemed as though there was no way whatsoever to escape the flood. But God had called a man to prepare a way out. Those who accepted God's way were delivered; those who did not were drowned in the catastrophe.

The world is not our source of provision and blessing.

Even though Lot was backslidden and had lost his way in God, he was still part of the covenant family. The covenant God had cut with Abraham extended to Lot and his family. When the judgment of God was finally about to fall upon Sodom and Gomorrah, angels from heaven came to rescue Lot from the coming doom.

Lot attempted to rescue his family as well, but his witness had become so weak through a heavily compromised lifestyle that he had no influence over his family. He was even hesitant about leaving the city he had fallen in love with. As he and his family left the city, they were warned not even to look back. However, Lot's wife pined for her life back in Sodom. She turned to watch as the city was destroyed. Lot and his daughters kept going, but his wife turned into a pillar of salt.

Remaining in Christ means staying free from the world. Christ gives us the power to separate ourselves from the world. As we remain focused on Him, we are set free from its enticements. It no longer chains us to either its pleasures or its pains.

God establishes the fact that His people are separated from the world as much through blessing as through protection from disasters. God does wonders among His people that no other group on earth experience.

> *Then the LORD said: "I am making a covenant with you. Before all your people I will do wonders never before done in any nation in all the world. The people you live among will see how awesome is the work that I, the LORD, will do for you."*
>
> EXODUS 34:10 NIV

We don't have to accept the plagues that come on the earth!

> *A thousand may fall at your side,*
> *And ten thousand at your right hand;*
> *But it shall not come near you.*
>
> PSALM 91:7

God works through miraculous means to supply His people when the rest of the world is struggling.

It is amazing how many Christians think that if there is disaster happening in the world then it must be going to affect them. If a financial recession comes upon the world, we don't have to join it! We are of a kingdom not of this world. The world is not our source of provision and blessing. God will always find a way for us to be blessed, even when the world is in trouble.

God directed Elijah to the brook Cherith when Israel was suffering famine (1 Kings 17:3). He commanded ravens to feed the prophet at the brook. Ravens are one of the most selfish of creatures, unwilling to share with another anything they've discovered. Yet God so altered their nature that every morning and evening they brought food they had found to the man of God. This was a miraculous provision that He afforded His servant.

After some time the brook Cherith dried up in the drought, and Elijah received instruction to move on to a town called Zarephath, where he was told a widow would provide for him. When Elijah arrived at Zarephath, however, he discovered the widow herself was about to die from starvation. She had absolutely no food except for a handful of wheat.

Elijah told her to give him the last of her food. She obeyed, and her generosity triggered the release of abundance so that throughout the rest of the famine neither she, nor her family, nor the prophet went without. God works through miraculous means to supply His people when the rest of the world is struggling.

> Remaining in Christ means we go where we are commanded to go so God can provide for us and protect us from what is going on in the world.

Unfortunately, much of the time the Christian church has looked like it needed to be set free from itself. It has looked like the world is enjoying prosperity, having much more fun, and generally getting along a lot better than those who are in Christ. This impression is from the devil. If we imagine we are meant to be struggling through life, we will never be a great witness for Christ. And yet many imagine it is more godly to suffer the troubles of this age than to be living in victory! This is not just about reaching lost people for Christ, either; it is also about keeping those who have decided to follow Jesus in the kingdom.

Many Christians become discouraged simply because they are laboring to get on in life with reasonable success but are hamstrung by false conceptions of what Christ expects of us. Many have been taught that prosperity is wrong, that holiness means being out of date and out of touch with life, and that we have to commit intellectual suicide in order to follow Jesus. A Christian might embrace these concepts for a brief time, but eventually they will discover the incredible difficulties of living in the world while holding such misguided beliefs.

Much of Christian thinking is simply inherited culture. When the Christian community overlays its culture as a requirement for holiness, then people are manipulated through guilt into living a very uncomfortable—and ultimately impossible lifestyle. Over time they slip away from Christ, not realizing that the standards they were trying to keep were not from the Lord in the first place.

Elijah simply obeyed God and went exactly where He told him to go. Over a period of three and a half years the prophet received divine provision first by the ravens and later by a widow. Both occasions were miraculous because the world did not dictate his destiny. God did.

Remaining in Christ means we go where we are commanded to go so God can provide for us and protect us from what is going on in the world. Being in Christ means we are set free from the world and all the curses to which it is subject.

"It is written."

Luke 4:4

9

Declare God's Word

For God has not given us a spirit of fear, but of power and of love and of a sound mind.

2 Timothy 1:7

So Jesus answered and said to them, "Have faith in God."

Mark 11:22

"I am the Lord who heals you."

Exodus 15:26

"He Himself took our infirmities and bore our sicknesses."

Matthew 8:17

For verily I say unto you, That whosoever shall say unto this mountain, Be thou removed, and be thou cast into the sea; and shall not doubt in his heart, but shall believe that those things which he saith shall come to pass; he shall have whatsoever he saith.

MARK 11:23 KJV

Therefore I say unto you, What things soever ye desire, when ye pray, believe that ye receive them, and ye shall have them.

MARK 11:24 KJV

Let us hold fast the profession of our faith without wavering; (for he is faithful that promised).

HEBREWS 10:23 KJV

"Fear not, for I have redeemed you;

I have called you by your name;

You are Mine.

When you pass through the waters, I will be with you;

And through the rivers, they shall not overflow you.

When you walk through the fire, you shall not be burned,

Nor shall the flame scorch you."

ISAIAH 43:1-2

Fear not, nor be dismayed; to morrow go out against them: for the LORD will be with you.

2 CHRONICLES 20:17 KJV

My God shall supply all your need according to His riches in glory by Christ Jesus.

PHILIPPIANS 4:19

I can do all things through Christ who strengthens me.

PHILIPPIANS 4:13

"With God all things are possible."

MATTHEW 19:26

"For with God nothing will be impossible."

LUKE 1:37

Now thanks be to God who always leads us in triumph in Christ.

2 CORINTHIANS 2:14

God, who quickeneth the dead, and calleth those things which be not as though they were.

ROMANS 4:17 KJV

"And whatever you ask in My name, that I will do."

JOHN 14:13

"Ask, and it will be given to you; seek, and you will find; knock, and it will be opened to you."

MATTHEW 7:7

This Book of the Law shall not depart from your mouth, but you shall meditate in it day and night, that you may observe to do according to all that is written in it. For then you will make your way prosperous, and then you will have good success.

JOSHUA 1:8

"If you abide in Me, and My words abide in you, you will ask what you desire, and it shall be done for you.

JOHN 15:7

"If you ask anything in My Name, I will do it."

JOHN 14:14

Blessed **is** *the man*

    Who walks not in the counsel of the ungodly,

    Nor stands in the path of sinners,

    Nor sits in the seat of the scornful;

But his delight **is** *in the law of the* LORD,

    And in His law he meditates day and night.

He shall be like a tree

    Planted by the rivers of water,

    That brings forth its fruit in its season,

    Whose leaf also shall not wither;

    And whatever he does shall prosper.

PSALM 1:1-3

Now faith is the substance of things hoped for, the evidence of things not seen.

HEBREWS 11:1

"And whatever things you ask in prayer, believing, you will receive."

MATTHEW 21:22

Beloved, I wish above all things that thou mayest prosper and be in health, even as thy soul prospereth.

3 JOHN 2 KJV

For whatever is born of God overcomes the world. And this is the victory that has overcome the world—our faith.

1 JOHN 5:4

Greater is he that is in you, than he that is in the world.

1 JOHN 4:4 KJV

"No weapon formed against you shall prosper."

ISAIAH 54:17

"Do not be afraid; you will not suffer shame.

Do not fear disgrace; you will not be humiliated."

ISAIAH 54:4 NIV

All your children shall be taught by the LORD,

And great shall be the peace of your children.

ISAIAH 54:13

Be anxious for nothing, but in everything by prayer and supplication, with thanksgiving, let your requests be made known to God.

PHILIPPIANS 4:6

Cast your burden on the LORD,

And He shall sustain you.

PSALM 55:22

Delight yourself also in the LORD,

And He shall give you the desires of your heart.

PSALM 37:3

Commit your way to the LORD;

trust in him and he will do this.

PSALM 37:5 NIV

"All things are possible to him who believes."

MARK 9:23

And we know that all things work together for good to those who love God, to those who are the called according to His purpose.

ROMANS 8:28

"I will never leave you nor forsake you."

HEBREWS 13:5

Prayer of Salvation

God loves you—no matter who you are, no matter what your past. God loves you so much that He gave His one and only begotten Son for you. The Bible tells us that "Whoever believes in him shall not perish but have eternal life" (John 3:16 NIV). Jesus laid down His life and rose again so that we could spend eternity with Him in heaven and experience His absolute best on earth. If you would like to receive Jesus into your life, say the following prayer out loud and mean it from your heart.

Heavenly Father, I come to You admitting that I am a sinner. Right now, I choose to turn away from sin, and I ask You to cleanse me of all unrighteousness. I believe that Your Son, Jesus, died on the Cross to take away my sins. I also believe that He rose again from the dead so that I might be forgiven of my sins and made righteous through faith in Him. I call upon the name of Jesus Christ to be the Savior and Lord of my life. Jesus, I choose to follow You and ask that You fill me with the power of the Holy Spirit. I declare that right now I am a child of God. I am free from sin and full of the righteousness of God. I am saved in Jesus' name. Amen.

If you prayed this prayer to receive Jesus Christ as your Savior for the first time, please contact us on the Web at **www.harrisonhouse.com** to receive a free book.

Or you may write to us at

Harrison House
P.O. Box 35035
Tulsa, Oklahoma 74153

About the Author

Pastor Phil Pringle is the Senior Minister of one of Australia's fastest growing, exciting, and powerful churches. In 1980 Phil and his wife, Christine, arrived in Sydney, Australia, from New Zealand, armed with faith and a vision to build a contemporary, vibrant church that would grow and impact a city for Christ.

Today, twenty-three years later, Christian City Church in Oxford Falls is one of Australia's largest churches with over four thousand members—quickly heading toward five thousand members. The church is made up of many departments, each reflecting Pastor Phil's original passion to liberate a city and nation through the life-transforming Gospel of Jesus Christ through every available relevant means.

Pastor Phil has always projected the vision of planting new congregations, especially in major cities around the world. Today Dr. Pringle oversees the approximately 1,200 churches that make up Christian City Church International throughout the world, a significant proportion of which have been planted directly from Christian City Church Oxford Falls.

Christian City Church Oxford Falls has a School of Ministry, developing powerful ministries for the future; a School of Creative Arts, developing ministries in the arts; Pastoral Care and Counseling College; the International School of the Church, which trains pastors and teams to plant churches and take the churches to new levels of growth; a business course; Jesus Television, a television studio creating high-quality material for weekly broadcasts; Seam of Gold, a record label, producing and distributing worldwide original and contemporary praise and worship coming out of this congregation.

The keys to this growth are vision, faith, moving in the Spirit, and development of leadership. Phil is a pastor, preacher, songwriter, artist, author, and leader. He maintains an uncompromised passion to see cities changed by a contemporary, relevant, and anointed church of God; and he shares his message in a down-to-earth manner, using humor and a sensitivity to the dynamics of the Holy Spirit.

In his meetings Pastor Phil has seen powerful moves of God break out, the glory of God filling the atmosphere, and people touched by the Holy Spirit. As a result, many have been saved and lives have been totally changed.

To contact Phil Pringle please write to:
Pax Ministries
Locked Bag 8
Dee Why NSW 2099
AUSTRALIA
Email: **pax@ccc.org.au**

*Please include your prayer requests
and comments when you write.*

Other Books by Dr. Pringle

Faith

Moving in the Spirit and the Anointing

Healing the Wounded Spirit

You the Leader

Keys to Financial Excellence

The Leadership Files Vol. 1

The Leadership Files Vol. 2

Books by Chris Pringle

Jesse—Found in Heaven

Additional copies of this book available at
www.harrisonhouse.com

Develop Qualities That Count

Dr. Phil Pringle, with more than 30 years experience in leadership and overseer of 200 churches worldwide, reveals 10 qualities that will empower you to lead effectively and teaches how to craft the strengths that great leaders posses. You will discover proven principles that will help you develop solid, lasting leadership qualities.

Hear what others are saying about this book:

One thing is for sure, this world needs leaders who operate with excellence! Dr. Pringle's **Top 10 Qualities of a Great Leader** *aims at the heart of a leader, giving you both spiritual and practical insights that will radically change the way you lead.*

—Joyce Meyer
Joyce Meyer Ministries
Fenton, Missouri

One of the clearest, most biblical works on leadership I have ever read. Reading it motivated me to go to the next level....

—Bill Hybels
Willow Creek Community Church

Phil Pringle's outstanding leadership skills have been proven over many years, and so he is well qualified to write this exceptional book on leadership.

—Brian Houston
General Superintendent,
Assemblies of God Australia/Senior Minister
Hillsong Church, Sydney, Australia

Top 10 Qualities of a Great Leader
Dr. Phil Pringle
ISBN-13: 978-1-57794-913-8

Available at bookstores everywhere
or visit **www.harrisonhouse.com**